TALES FROM THE MEMPHIS GRIZZLIES HARDWOOD

Ron Higgins

SP
SPORTS
PUBLISHING
L.L.C.

SportsPublishingLLC.com

ISBN-10: 1-59670-020-3
ISBN-13: 978-1-59670-020-8

Publishers: Peter L. Bannon and Joseph J. Bannon Sr.
Senior managing editor: Susan M. Moyer
Acquisitions editor: John Humenik
Developmental editor: Travis W. Moran
Art director: K. Jeffrey Higgerson
Dust jacket design: Dustin J. Hubbart
Interior layout: Kathryn R. Holleman
Photo editor: Erin Linden-Levy

Sports Publishing L.L.C.
804 North Neil Street
Champaign, IL 61820
Phone: 1-877-424-2665
Fax: 217-363-2073
SportsPublishingLLC.com

Printed in the United States of America

   Library of Congress Cataloging-in-Publication Data

Higgins, Ron, 1956-
   Tales from the Memphis Grizzlies hardwood / Ron Higgins.
      p. cm.
   ISBN-13: 978-1-59670-020-8 (hardcover : alk. paper)
   ISBN-10: 1-59670-020-3 (hardcover : alk. paper)
   1. Memphis Grizzlies (Basketball team) 2. Basketball--Tennessee--Memphis. I.
Title.
   GV885.52.M46H54 2006
   796.323'640976819--dc22
                          2006028409

FOR MY BEAUTIFUL WIFE, PAIGE, AND RELATIVELY PATIENT SONS, CARL AND JACK, WHO HAVE ALWAYS BEEN SUPPORTIVE IN MY LONG, WINDING, AND NOT EXACTLY LUCRATIVE SPORTS-WRITING CAREER.

FOR MY LATE FATHER, ACE, WHO GAVE ME THE GIFT OF WRITING AND THE LOVE OF SPORTS, AND FOR MY MOTHER, PAT, WHO NEVER THINKS I WRITE A BAD STORY.

FOR FORMER GRIZ COACH HUBIE BROWN, WHOSE PASSION AND WORK ETHIC MAKE ME LOOK FORWARD TO BEING 70 AND BEYOND. AND FOR LATE GRIZ PLAY-BY-PLAY VOICE DON POIER, WHO LOVED THE GRIZ ALMOST AS MUCH AS HE LOVED HIS WIFE, BARB.

CONTENTS

ACKNOWLEDGMENTS

Many thanks to my book editor, Travis Moran, who talked me down off the ledge a time or two, and to John Humenik (formerly known as the best college sports information director in America), who encouraged me to take on this project.

Thanks as well to the Grizzlies—particularly media relations director Stacey Mitch (who keeps Starbucks in business) and her staff of Graham Kendrick (who came from Vancouver and lasted a lot longer than Big Country) and Ryan Deady, team president of business Andy Dolich, and former team vice president of business Mike Golub.

Thanks to Griz forward Shane Battier for writing the foreword that didn't make the book since he was traded to Houston (sorry Shane!), and thanks for his consistently sensible perspective season after season. Thanks to former Grizzlies coach Hubie Brown, the best teacher in the history of basketball, who took me to the classroom every time he answered one of my questions.

Thanks to my first boss in the business in 1980, Gerry Robichaux of *The Shreveport (Louisiana) Times* for giving me the freedom to grow, and to my sports editors over the years at *The (Memphis) Commercial Appeal*, Lon Eubanks, Walter Veazey, John Stamm, and finally, Gary Robinson, for putting me in the right places at the right times. Thanks to my closest friends in the business, John "Wag" Adams, Joe "Mr." Biddle, Jim "FOB" Mashek, Tommy "L'il P" Hicks, and Jimmy "Silk Blend" Hyams for their advice and friendship throughout the years.

FROM BRITISH COLUMBIA TO BLUFF CITY

MEMPHIS IN THE NBA? REALLY?

The average Memphis sports fan thought the city's chance to get a major professional sports franchise had sailed away in the 1990s, when the city made a hard push to get an NFL expansion franchise. But the league owners—noting that Memphis wasn't willing to build a new stadium to replace the outdated Liberty Bowl—awarded franchises to Charlotte and Jacksonville.

Memphis took the defeat hard, having felt it done all the right things to get a franchise. The city had held exhibition game after exhibition game as it was urged to sell out stadiums, because supposedly the NFL owners were watching to see if Memphis would support a team.

It had put together a solid ownership group, featuring FedEx founder Fred Smith, and cotton merchant Billy Dunavant, who had been the majority owner of the successful Memphis Showboats of the United States Football League in the '80s.

So when the NFL said "No," Memphis was angry. When the Houston Oilers announced that they were leaving Houston to move to Nashville in 1997, the rapier cut deeper. The blade was jabbed even further when the new Tennessee team, called the Titans, spent one of their seasons in Memphis while their new stadium was being built.

Since the American Basketball Association went out of business in the mid-1970s, Memphis hadn't had a major pro basketball team. Every minor league seemed to try a team in Memphis—the Rockers, the Fire, the HotShots, the Houn' Dawgs—they all came and went in the 1990s.

Almost every franchise tried the premise of getting some former University of Memphis players as a gate attraction. The public, though— even with cheap ticket prices—never hopped on board. They wanted a real, honest-to-goodness, major professional franchise. They were tired of second-rate.

OH, CANADA

By the 2001 All-Star break, the players of the Vancouver Grizzlies had heard the rumors. They might be moving at season's end.

Team owner Michael Heisley, a Chicago businessman who bought the team in April 2000 for $160 million, looked at having an NBA team in a Canadian city as a financial drain, losing an estimated $46 to $50 million in 2000-01, their sixth and final year.

"I'm not going to sit here and eat double-digit dollars for a long period of time, I'll tell you that," said Heisley before the season opener against Seattle. "But if people don't think I wouldn't like to make this a success in Vancouver, then they are idiots."

That might seem a bit harsh, but Heisley is a no-nonsense guy. In fact, a group of Memphians called the "NBA Pursuit Team," which had operated in secret for more than a year in seeking a team for the city, saw how quickly Heisley got involved in a possible relocation.

The Charlotte Hornets had already been talking with the pursuit team for several months. Hornets co-owner Ray Woolridge, a native Memphian, even toured The Pyramid, Memphis' downtown basketball arena, on November 1, 2000.

Just more than three months later when NBA Commissioner David Stern gave his blessing to start shopping for a new home, it took Heisley less than two weeks to call Memphis Mayor Willie Herenton.

Heisley basically told Herenton, "We're the only team being re-located, and if you want an NBA team, you better talk to me."

A day later, Heisley made his first visit to Memphis incognito, and the flame had been ignited.

"I never considered the franchise a laughingstock, I just thought it needed a lot of work," said Heisley, who built a career at turning downtrodden companies into profitable enterprises. "I enjoy the challenge of turning companies around. I was very fortunate to pick Memphis, and it wasn't a surefire thing."

MEANWHILE, NORTH OF THE BORDER

So as Heisley met behind the scenes with Memphis city and county officials, the Grizzlies played out their final days. Griz players had mixed emotions.

They loved the fact that Vancouver was a cosmopolitan city of two million people, with some of the most breathtaking scenery one could find. But even that couldn't outweigh the feeling the Grizzlies were insignificant in the Great White North.

"Basketball isn't the No. 1 thing in Canada," said forward Shareef Abdur-Rahim, the team's best player. "When we go on the road to Indianapolis and walk through a mall as a team, we get more attention from those people who want to talk to us about basketball than we do here in Vancouver.

"I can't say everything here [in Vancouver] has been great; but if we leave, we'll leave a lot of good people I care about.

"There's more good than bad in a move. If we go to a new city like Memphis—a city that's wanted a pro franchise—those fans might be so glad just to have a team that they might view us like an expansion franchise. They might not expect us to win for two or three years.

"But I want to win now," Shareef proclaimed. "I don't want to be in a situation where I feel we're not expected to win. We need to get some players who can contribute now. We can't afford to wait on anybody.

THE LAST HURRAH

The day before the Grizzlies' final home game in history in Vancouver, no local media attended the practice. The last home game before a crowd of 18,571 on April 18, 2001, was a 100-95 loss to Houston. The video replay board played highlights of the team's six-year stay.

Some of the Griz faithful held signs in the stands that read, "Vancouver 4-Ever, Memphis Never," "Goodbye Cruel Game," and "I No Longer Love This Game." It was an emotional night for Abdur-Rahim and Bryant Reeves, the cornerstones of the franchise.

"Knowing that I helped get this franchise started, I'm proud to be the only [original] player left here," Reeves said. "There were a lot of years here I had fun. It would have meant everything to win this last game."

Added Abdur-Rahim, "When I came here, I was 19 years old [drafted after his freshman season at the University of California], and I didn't know what to expect. This city embraced me. I guess growing up as a kid, you always watched other teams, and they had guys who stayed on one team their whole career. You remembered their names and the color of their uniforms. Magic [Johnson] played in purple and gold for the Lakers. Isiah [Thomas] played in red and blue for the Pistons. The way you dream it, the way you paint it, is to go with one team, win with that team, and retire in the city."

Veteran forward Grant Long put the move in perspective. "No one on this team has ever been involved in a team relocation. It's a lot different than just a player being traded. It's like the whole team being traded."

REGRETS ... HEISLEY HAD A FEW

Heisley has always said he didn't feel bad about moving the franchise to Memphis, but he was disappointed that the franchise didn't work in Vancouver.

"The people in Vancouver welcomed us like the people in Memphis," Heisley said. "The people in Vancouver are great people. But I lost a horrendous amount of money the first year I owed the team. Season ticket sales went down, and a lot of commitments had been made to the NBA about corporate ticket sales. I finally realized I wasn't going to be successful. Vancouver was in a recession and they had two major sports teams in hockey and basketball. It's tough to spend thousands of dollars on both, and Vancouver is a big outdoors town. The place wasn't big enough for us and the Canucks [hockey].

"I felt very comfortable about moving," Heisley added. "We didn't own the building, and we were paying millions each year for rent. We got no concession revenue from the building. We got paid in Canadian, and I had to pay the players in American, and the exchange rate was 64 cents to the dollar. I almost felt I was forced into the decision to move."

HOW BAD IS BAD

Memphis was getting quite possibly the worst franchise in pro sports. They lost 100, 200, and 300 games faster than any franchise in NBA history. When the Griz left Vancouver, they were 101-359. They had six straight losing seasons, five head coaches, three owners, and no playoff berths.

Yet, there was a glimmer of hope, because four of the team's top seven players were 25 years old or younger. Then-Orlando Magic general manager John Gabriel waxed prophetic when assessing the Grizzlies' chances to become successful.

"What any franchise needs is leadership," Gabriel said. "It might come in the form of a general manager, like the Jerry Wests [who rebuilt the Los Angeles Lakers] of the world."

Jerry West come to Memphis? Who was Gabriel kidding?

THE CHICKEN BEFORE THE EGG

By mid-May, as Heisley negotiated a contract with the city and the county, the Grizzlies had an administrative team in the city looking at practice sites and office space. Part of the package involved the construction of a new $250 million downtown arena to open by the third season.

On the night of the NBA lottery, prospective fans of new Memphis Grizzlies packed a sports bar in East Memphis called the Fox and Hound to get the chance to meet general manager Billy Knight, coach Sidney Lowe, and Abdur-Rahim.

"Billy tried to tell me about Memphis because he came here before, but the people have been tremendous and upbeat," Lowe said. "It makes you want to be here. These people follow basketball. They even remember me when I played in college [as a guard on North Carolina State's 1983 national championship team]."

Abdur-Rahim was excited about the prospect of living in Memphis, having already scouted downtown for a Mississippi River waterfront home. "Being in Vancouver, all the players usually packed up and moved back to their U.S. homes at the end of the season," he said. "Playing in Memphis will give us the opportunity to live here after a season is over and be a part of the community."

HELLO, LORENZEN

Just days before the Grizzlies' first draft—with the league approval pending for a move to Memphis—Griz general manager Billy Knight promised "we will have a drastically different roster than last year, and that's even if we don't do any trades."

Guess what? The night before the draft, Knight traded Abdur-Rahim to the Atlanta Hawks for Atlanta's No. 3 pick, as well as former University of Memphis center Lorenzen Wright, and point guard Brevin Knight.

The move gave the Griz five draft choices, including three in the first round at Nos. 3, 6, and 27.

"Hands down, this is the best day of my life," Wright said less than 12 hours after the trade. "Everyone in my family is happy. I didn't think this was possible, because I didn't think the Grizzlies would ever trade Shareef. I'm so blessed."

Lorenzen should have listened to his father, Herb. A couple of days before the draft, Herb told his son, "I heard the Grizzlies are going to trade Shareef for you."

PAU, MEET SHANE ... SHANE, MEET PAU

On a hot June day in New York City before the 2001 NBA draft, Pau Gasol and Shane Battier sat just a few feet apart at tables in a Manhattan hotel meeting room, talking with media about their draft chances. Gasol's table was full of international media, especially from Spain, where the

Former Griz center Lorenzen Wright saves an old friend, NBA referee Michael Smith of Memphis. © 2005 NBA Entertainment. Photo by Joe Murphy.

young Gasol was the hot up-and-coming star. Battier's table had American media, familiar with his four-year heroics at Duke where, as college basketball's best player, he was fresh off helping his team win the national championship.

"I'd seen one Final Four game that Shane played," Gasol said.

"All I knew of Pau was when I read his name on the draft board," Battier said.

The next night, within the span of an hour, they became teammates. Gasol was picked No. 3 by Atlanta and sent to the Griz in the Lorenzen Wright-Brevin Knight trade; and Memphis chose Battier at No. 6.

Gasol, a baby-faced 20-year-old, was dazzled by the proceedings. He was the first foreigner ever taken by the Griz. "This is my first time in the States, and I'm the third pick in the draft," he said. "It is all going very fast for me. New York is big—big buildings, a lot of people. People go crazy here."

Being drafted No. 3 was key for Gasol. Since there was a buyout of his F.C. Barcelona contract—a $2.5 million transfer fee since there were two years left on his contract, he had to be drafted high enough to make it worth his while.

"I didn't have any clue who would draft me," Gasol said. "But I knew if I wasn't in the first six picks or so, I would have stayed one more year in Spain and come to the league the next year without paying my buyout. But then my agent told me when Atlanta made that trade that Memphis might be interested. When they picked me, it was shocking, and it was great. I think my adjustment to the league will be tough, but I will give all my effort to make the adjustment as quick as possible."

LATE NIGHT WITH J-WILL

The hubbub surrounding the Abdur-Rahim trade before the draft and the selections of Gasol and Battier overshadowed an important late-night trade that sent Mike Bibby and Brent Price to Sacramento for Jason Williams and Nick Anderson.

The trade for Williams was a stunner, especially since he had languished on Sacramento's bench in the fourth quarter of playoff games due to his tendency to play out of control. But Dick Versace, the

Grizzlies' director of basketball operations, had talked to Williams previously and liked him.

"I just had a connection with Jason when I interviewed him," Versace said. "Now, I thought he was a character. But I liked him and I loved his foot speed—I'm a speed-and-shooting junkie—and we desperately needed speed at the point. I gave up shooting [in Bibby] for speed. I also felt in the first year here that Jason would help us sell tickets."

Williams had baggage. He played just 48 games in college at Marshall (1995-96) and Florida (1997-98), before being kicked off the team at Florida for testing positive for marijuana. He was drafted No. 7 overall by Sacramento in the '98 draft, and finished second in Rookie of the Year voting. But in a rocky 2000-01 season, Williams served a five-game NBA suspension for not complying with the league's drug treatment policy after testing positive for marijuana, and was fined $45,000 for three courtside incidents with fans.

When Kings Coach Rick Adelman began cutting Williams' playing time in the fourth quarter of games, tired of his poor shot selection and sometimes showboat passing, J-Will began looking for the exit.

"I didn't ask to be traded, it was more of a suggestion," Williams said. "I thought it would be best for me, because Coach Adelman and I weren't on the same page for some reason. There were some things he did as a coach that I didn't agree with, and I'm sure there are some things I did as a player he didn't agree with. It was like two bullheads colliding. Not a lot of coaches will let me play the way I'm capable of playing. I'm grateful that I now have a coach [Sidney Lowe] that will allow me to play that way."

As it turned out, the cuddly feelings lasted about as long as Williams' initial press conference.

THE EXPRESS LINE

As the NBA gave its approval on the Grizzlies' move to Memphis on June 28, 2001, there was talk that the team may change its nickname to Express—possibly a tie-in from FedEx, which had made a substantial naming offer on the proposed new arena.

Majority owner Michael Heisley said he liked the Express nickname, and he didn't consider it a corporate tie-in to FedEx. (The NBA doesn't allow corporations to be used as nicknames.) "I like the name," he said, "but if the marketing people don't feel that's a good name for us to use, then I don't think we'd use it."

A LONG SEASON

Wins came far and few between in the Grizzlies' first season in Memphis. But even with a revolving door of guards late in the season, Memphis won its last 6-of-13 games to finish 23-59, tying the franchise records for wins.

"That first year it was hard to win a game," Griz center Lorenzen Wright just before the start of the '05-'06 season. "Then, when we won and got to the playoffs, fans wanted to know when we're going to win a playoff game. When we do that, it'll be 'When are you guys going to get to the second round?'"

2

OLE' PAU

¡HOLA, SEÑOR GASOL!

The day before the 2001 NBA draft, in a crowded meeting room in a downtown New York City, media hovered around the top draft prospects who would soon become millionaires. High school stars Kwame Brown, Eddy Curry, and Tyson Chandler, were talking about what they planned to buy when that first paycheck full of zeroes landed in their laps. There was Duke star Shane Battier, the college player of the year on the national championship team, talking about feeling a bit out of place—he was probably the only player in the room who had stayed in college all four years.

Then, there was this skinny foreign guy from Spain, looking every bit the wide-eyed 20-year-old, surrounded by Spanish reporters jabbering a mile a minute. His name was Pau Gasol, and he had created a buzz in the European basketball community as seven-foot, 227-pound talent who could run the floor, shoot with range, and finish around the basket with either hand. He had just finished a breakout season with F.C. Barcelona, where he was the Most Valuable Player of the Copa del Ray (the Spanish

National Cup), and MVP of the ACB Finals—the top Spanish pro league.

Until Gasol looked in the stands and saw NBA scouts eyeing and furiously scribbling notes, he hadn't realized that basketball might take him on a journey that he had never imagined. "When the scouts came to see me play in Spain," he said, "I realize that I had the ability to come to the NBA and play."

Walter Szczerbiak, a representative of the ACB league, said Gasol's skills and versatility made him a tough matchup. "You can't defend him with a '3' [a small forward], because he's just too tall," said Szczerbiak. "If you defend him with a bigger guy, he'll drive around you. He has a variety of post moves and he plays with heart."

For those reasons, Gasol caught the attention of then-Griz General Manager Billy Knight and Player Personnel Director Tony Barone. They traveled to Europe to confirm what they had seen the previous year before an F.C. Barcelona game.

"We watched him warm up, and what we saw was a seven-footer who could handle the ball like a guard, and someone who could shoot hook shots with either hand," Barone said. "We put him on our list to come back and see him the next year. The next year, we saw him play three times. He had tremendous athleticism. He could take defenders off the dribble and dunk, and he could pass. He was clever, quick and cute around the paint, but still a little raw offensively. He had a slow jump shot, and the release wasn't that great. But you could tell that, when he got strong and matured, all of that would improve."

Because Gasol was still involved in his season, he never worked out individually for any NBA team prior to the draft. That didn't matter to the Grizzlies. They liked what they had seen. Late the night before the draft, Knight completed the aforementioned deal that sent the Grizzlies' all-time leading scorer, Shareef Abdur-Rahim, to the Atlanta Hawks along with their No. 27 pick in exchange for the Hawks' No. 3 pick. Though history was against the Grizzlies drafting a foreign or high school player—they'd never chosen either in the 13 players they picked in six previous drafts—Knight made that trade because he wanted Gasol.

"Pau played at a high level of European basketball, [with] experience that a lot of 20-year-olds don't have," Knight explained.

When Knight got his man, instructing Atlanta to draft Gasol, Gasol became the highest international draft choice ever. Though Gasol had never been in a weight room—European coaches believe weight lifting ruins a player's shooting stroke—he was confident that his skills could translate to the NBA.

"I like Kevin Garnett [of the Timberwolves] because physically he's like me," Gasol said. "He's not strong, but he's a skinny guy who plays very, very well. He can shoot outside. He can post up."

To jump to the NBA, Gasol had to pay a multimillion-dollar transfer fee to his Spanish team, because he had two years left on his contract. Memphis was able to pay $350,000 of the transfer.

"I wanted to play in the best league in the world," Gasol said, "so if I [have to] pay the money, I [will] pay the money."

A NATIONAL HERO

All it takes to realize that Gasol's status in Spain grows each passing season is to understand several things. First, there's the number of hits on the Griz website from foreign locales. Secondly, Griz Media Relations Director Stacey Mitch is kept hopping by a stream of visiting Spanish and European reporters that started in Gasol's first ever regular-season NBA game (also the first ever in Memphis) on November 1, 2001.

Back then, a contingent of Spanish reporters—as well as 150 Spaniards—made the trip to see Gasol's pro debut.

In a 90-80 loss to the Pistons, he didn't start the game, but he entered with 3:35 left in the first quarter, and scored the first points of his pro career with 6:10 left in the second quarter as he dunked after taking a pass from Jason Williams. He finished with four points, four rebounds, and four turnovers.

Even now, Gasol's Spanish national team jersey is sold in the Griz gift shop at the FedExForum. During the 2005-06 season, the Griz honored Gasol with a Spanish Night promotion for which everyone who could prove they were born in Spain received free admission to the game. That same game, the Grizzlies passed out fake paper beards for fans to wear, honoring Gasol's beard that he grew for the season.

When Gasol didn't play for the Spanish team in the summer of '05—he declined so he could fully recover from his plantar-fasciitis foot problems that sidelined him for more than a month during the '04-'05 season—it was big news all over Spain.

It was a tough decision for Gasol, who was the leading scorer (22.4 points) of the 2004 Athens Olympics for 6-1 Spain, which finished sixth. Though the rest helped him in '05-'06, he promised he would return to play for Spain in the summer of '06.

"I know how good it makes me feel to be in that environment," Gasol said. "It's something that keeps me connected to my country, it keeps me tight with my fans. It's special for me. I know it's not the best-case scenario for me to go into an NBA season having played in the summer; but Dirk Nowitzki [from Germany] and [the Spurs'] Tony Parker [from France] have done the same thing every year and have played excellent. I think it's a matter of being mentally strong enough to put the summer behind you and refresh yourself for the [NBA] season."

When Gasol and the Grizzlies played some exhibitions in Spain prior to the '03-'04 season, it was like Elvis had come home. At a photo shoot at Footlocker, 1,000 fans waited to have their pictures snapped with him. To those people, one of their own—the son of Agustin and Marisa, high school basketball players who became a doctor and a nurse, respectively—had achieved the dream of becoming an NBA star.

Gasol, who had blonde hair as a youngster, lived with his family in the Barcelona suburb of Sant Boi. He attended Escola Llor, a private school where he tried to balance school, basketball, and piano lessons. Pau began playing basketball when he was six and grew up playing all five positions. When he was 13, he had a coach who made him play point guard so he could improve his court vision. He went from measuring 6-feet-4 as a 16-year-old to about seven feet between his 18th and 19th birthdays.

Gasol drew his basketball inspiration from the NBA. He watched live telecasts of future Hall of Famers Magic Johnson of the Lakers and Larry Bird of the Celtics, and loved their games.

"I admired and idolized Magic and Bird, because they were so sure and so confident of themselves, so calm," Gasol said. "They had a real feel of the game. I also liked Toni Kukoc [a 6-foot-11 forward from Croatia] when he joined the Bulls [in 1993]. Everybody loved Kukoc because he got a chance to play on an NBA championship team."

ROOKIE OF THE YEAR

Gasol may have never gotten a chance to start early in his rookie season if second-year forward Stromile Swift hadn't been sidelined with an ankle injury. Gasol was playing behind Swift when he was injured at a shoot-around in Phoenix prior to the team's fifth exhibition game.

"I'd struggled in my first four games, so when Stro got hurt, I got a chance to play a lot of minutes in Phoenix, and that gave me more confidence," Gasol said.

It took a while that first season for Gasol and fellow rookie Shane Battier to get settled. Battier played in the summer league for the Griz, but Gasol had to get his contract settled in Spain before he could join the Grizzlies shortly before the start of training camp.

"I'd never seen Pau play until we scrimmaged in September before training camp," Battier said. "I'm like, 'Man, this kid is pretty good. We lucked out—we got a good one.' I don't think anyone could foresee Pau's rapid development. We got a very good one."

Gasol said his first month or so up to the season started was tough personally. He was just a 21-year-old kid far away from home in a new country for the first time in his life.

"I missed home so much," Gasol said. "I didn't know anybody here. My English wasn't that good, and I lived for a month in a hotel. My family came a month after I got here, and we rented a little apartment in Germantown. I knew my way from there to Pyramid, there to Rhodes [where the Grizzlies practice]. That's all I knew, and that's all I needed."

Gasol's original goal was to just fight for playing time. That quickly changed.

"I kept winning that Rookie of the Month, and that really motivated me," Gasol said. "And then I got Rookie of the Year."

WITH NOTORIETY COMES THE EXPECTATIONS

As in any sport, when an athlete wins an honor or reaches a goal, more is expected—fans want more. Coaches definitely want more, too, as

Perhaps the beard Grizzlies forward Pau Gasol sprouted in '05-'06 helped take his game to an all-star level. © 2006 NBA Entertainment. Photo by Joe Murphy

Hubie Brown proved when he took over as Grizzlies coach early in the '02-'03 season. Brown knew his job was to foster Gasol's growth as a player. It didn't take a genius to see Gasol was regarded as the cornerstone of the revitalized franchise; but there have been nights when the growing pains have been severe, such as the first half of a Grizzlies home game against the Warriors in early February 2004. Brown quickly lost patience after Warriors center Erick Dampier tipped in three offensive rebounds over Gasol by midway through the second quarter.

Brown angrily called time out and screamed at Gasol, "If you don't start jumping, I'm going to pull you out. If you don't jump, you can't rebound. If you can't rebound, you can't play."

Eventually, Lorenzen Wright went in the game and was on his way to an 18-point performance when Brown put Gasol back in the game with nine minutes left. The Memphis crowd started booing, and booed even louder a few minutes later as he held the ball too long in the post and was stripped, which led to a shot-clock violation.

"I didn't hear the boos," Gasol said afterward. "If I do, I hope they aren't booing me."

Brown understood the frustration of Griz fans. "There were five scores [by the Warriors] that Pau should have rebounded. Through that, you've got to be a hell of a fan to stay positive."

Just two games removed from that dead-on-arrival performance against the Warriors, Gasol began playing like the franchise's foundation. After a 20-point win against the Bucks in which he had 27 points, 12 rebounds, five blocked shots, and two steals, Brown said of Gasol, "He's a monster when he does that."

Gasol's play wasn't the most stunning part. He showed anger after teammate Mike Miller was slammed to the floor by Milwaukee's Desmond Mason in the second quarter. Mason called the collision an accident, but as Miller and his bad back crumpled in a heap facedown; Gasol raced to Mason and drew a technical when he got in his face—much to the surprise and delight of his teammates.

"Pau was the first one over there, telling Mason that it wasn't right; and early in his career, he wouldn't have done anything like that," Wright said.

Coincidentally, after Miller was helped off the floor for the rest of the night, Gasol scored eight of the Grizzlies' next 10 points, including two sweeping fast-break dunks off Jason Williams passes.

"I saw what happened [with Miller]. I just couldn't let him [Mason] go to the bench like that," Gasol said. "So I just stepped right in front of him and told him it was wrong. I was really upset the way he [Miller] went down, and I took that frustration out by running the court hard and taking it to the rim every time no matter what. From the first minute of the game, I concentrated on being more aggressive."

A few weeks later in a three-point win over the Nuggets, despite suffering what was termed a nasal fracture with 7:18 left in the first half, Gasol delivered 25 points and seven rebounds. Gasol, who had a bad habit of whining to the refs about non-foul calls, began shutting his mouth and playing.

"From Day One, I told Pau not to say anything to the refs, just play through it, and he'll get more respect," Griz point guard Jason Williams said.

Even after Gasol caught an elbow from Nuggets center Nene and was led to the locker room clutching his nose, there was never a doubt in his mind that he was going to come back and finish the job.

"I'm trying to be more mature about my game, trying to be even more aggressive," Gasol said. "I've learned it doesn't do me any good to talk to the refs. If I don't get a call, I just try harder to get one the next time."

Battier, joined at the hip with Gasol since they were selected by the Griz within minutes of each other in the first round of the '01 draft, said Gasol's maturity came to the forefront. "It seems like he came into the league and didn't have any adjustment period after he won Rookie of the Year. It was awkward for him, but he's finally settling into who he is. He's confident and taking his game to the opposition instead of the opposition taking it to him. He's finally getting respect from officials, but he's also making aggressive moves toward the basket. You couldn't always say that about his game."

Even in his fourth NBA season, in '04-'05, under his third different coach, Mike Fratello, Gasol was trying to reach a level of consistency that his coaches thought he should attain—as in the first game of the playoffs at Phoenix, a 114-103 loss. Fratello benched Gasol in the final half, playing a grand total of eight minutes. Gasol, who had 16 points, seven rebounds, and two blocked shots in 26 minutes of the opener, wasn't getting things done defensively to Fratello's liking.

Gasol, who missed 23 games during the 2004-05 regular season with plantar fasciitis in his left foot, felt that the Griz needed to counter by probing the Suns' supposed weakness—inside defense.

"We need to take advantage of my abilities to try hurt them," Gasol said. "They attack our weak points. We need to attack their weak points, attack their mismatches. They are doing what we're supposed to do."

Gasol may have raised eyebrows by hinting the offense needed to be run through him, but it's the way franchise players are supposed to act. Give them the ball, and they'll carry you. When Gasol had a double-double of 28 points and 16 rebounds in a 108-103 game two loss against the Suns, it marked another step forward in his career. But the real progress wouldn't come until the '05-'06 season.

YES, HE'S THE MAN

Before the start of the '04-'05 season, Gasol signed a six-year, $86-million deal that announced he was the player being deemed the foundation of the franchise.

"It's not about the money, it's about the respect," Gasol said when he signed. "I'm ready to be the cornerstone. I love that pressure."

Yet it wasn't until the '05-'06 season, when the Griz traded shoot-first point guard Jason Williams and decided to run the offense through Gasol in the low post, that Pau fully flourished. Gasol grew further and further from his early career persona of being stripped while shooting, then begging an official for a foul while the player he was supposed to defend beats him back to the offensive end for a basket.

Gasol was making quick decisions and finishing plays more often, with hooks, fadeaways, and vicious dunks. Sure, there were still nights where his rebounding was suspect, but it was obvious this was a different Gasol.

No Griz player benefited more in '05-'06 from the addition of free-agent point guard Damon Stoudamire more than Gasol. Gasol, still maturing in his game, received constant confidence boosts from Stoudamire—something previous point guards hadn't shown Gasol.

"I don't know what went on with Pau over the last couple of years, I've only heard," Stoudamire said. "I can only go on what I see. The first thing I tell Pau is, no matter how much he has been criticized by whoever, he has to come out and play hard every night.

"Because if he doesn't play hard every night for us, we can't win. I've played with many great players. I think he can get to that point. He has a chance to do that. If I had one critique of his game, I would like to see him work on his stamina in the summer. He needs to be able to go 38 or 39 minutes every night," Stoudamire added. "And that takes a lot when a guy leans on him all night. The top power forwards play 40 minutes a night. He needs to reach that level."

When Stoudamire tore a patella tendon on December 30 at the Trail Blazers, sidelining him for the rest of the season, Gasol turned up his game.

"With Damon out, Pau has taken a new role on for our team," Shane Battier said at the time. "He's become a facilitator that we run our offense through. Pau's playing at an all-star level. He's our rock."

Battier didn't hold back in urging the Grizzlies' fans to vote for Gasol, particularly after an early January win over the Jazz in which Gasol had 27 points, a career high-tying 18 rebounds, seven assists, and four blocked shots.

"Pau played a man's game," Battier said. "That's what a franchise player does. He gets an extra scoop of ice cream on the plane tonight. It would be ludicrous, the travesty of all travesties, if Pau was left off the [all-star] team. Now, more than ever, I urge people to get out there and exercise your right to vote. Vote NOW! Vote PAU!"

SO SHANE KNEW WHAT
HE WAS TALKING ABOUT

A few weeks after Battier talked about Pau's all-star level play, the Western Conference coaches agreed. They elected Gasol to a reserve spot on the West All-Star team—making Pau the first Grizzly to receive that honor.

What raised Gasol's game to an all-star level?

"I've been playing a lot of minutes, and I know I'm going to be on the floor," Gasol said. "My conditioning is good, and my confidence level is high. I get the ball in the post a lot, and I've gotten to read every type of defense. I'm being patient, reading the defense. I know when to attack, and know when to pass. I know that, when I get a lot of attention, I can create a lot for my teammates. I like this responsibility, and I've stepped up my game."

AND THERE WERE OTHER THEORIES

Everyone associated with Gasol on a daily basis had his or her own thoughts on why Pau's game exploded in his fifth season—why, for the first time in his career, he got stronger after the all-star break.

"There has been a maturity that has taken place in Pau's approach to the game," Griz Coach Mike Fratello said. "He has become more vocal, and he's accepted the responsibility that he has to be effective night in and night out if we're going to win. The natural thing for most international players who come into the NBA is a reluctance to try to take over a situation out of the respect of the people who are already here—especially if you're a young guy and there's people playing in front of you who have been in the league for eight or nine years. Pau is a good teammate. He's not going to come in and try to tread on anybody immediately.

"Like the natural evolution of a Dirk Nowitzki in Dallas, an international player grows into the game," Fratello continued. "They get to a point where they understand they have to become more involved. That's where Pau is right now."

Getting new veteran teammates, who showed confidence in him helped him, reach his potential.

"You don't know how good a guy is until you play with him," said point guard Chucky Atkins, who signed with the Griz as a free agent in January 2006. "I knew Pau could score points. Most guys who are starters on their teams, nine times out of 10, are selfish guys. Pau is totally the opposite. He plays to win games, which is to his credit."

Said Gasol, who finished the regular season averaging a career-high 20.4 points, 8.9 rebounds, 4.6 assists, and 39.2 minutes, "If I perform at a high level, we have a better chance to win. My teammates give me a lot of confidence. They tell me, 'Shoot 20 shots, shoot 30 shots—you're our man. You're our guy.'"

Most of the Grizzlies who were raised in the franchise with Gasol felt his decision not to play on the Spanish National Team in the summer before the '05-'06 season—the first summer he hadn't played on the team since he joined the Griz—gave him more energy all season.

"Every year when Pau came in at the start of the season, we could see that he'd be so tired," Griz center Lorenzen Wright said. "We'd always mention it to him that maybe he should sit out [and not play in the summer with the Spanish National team]. After sitting out last summer, when he got here in training camp, you could tell he was a lot more lively, just energetic, playful, jumping around, instead of coming in tired, banged up, and knowing he had 82 games in front of him."

"NOW, HE'S GOT ENERGY."

As much as Gasol loves playing for his country, he had to admit he didn't feel as drained during the '05-'06 season.

"Compared to the last couple of years, I'm fresher—much fresher than I was two years ago when I hurt my ankle late in the regular season. Then last year, as I tried to come back from my fasciitis, trying to get in shape and get in the rhythm of the game again," said Gasol a couple of weeks before the end of the regular season. "This year, it's a much better situation."

Even Griz majority owner Michael Heisley weighed in on Gasol's improvement. "I think people don't give Pau credit. People always say players who come from Europe are soft. Pau's not soft. I think he had a different style in Europe, playing in a situation where fouls are called. He grew up in that system, and he had to adjust playing here where he gets bumped every play. In Europe, those bumps are fouls. If we played the international brand of basketball here, he'd be an all-star every year and one of the most dominant players in the league.

"I think Pau realized this season ['05-'06] what he had to do," Heisley added. "He rested last summer, worked out, and put on some muscle. He came in with a lot more determination, and it has shown."

AND MAYBE IT WAS THE BEARD

Before the '05-'06 season, Gasol, back home in Spain, was so relaxed that he stopped shaving. Soon, there was a beard.

"I kind of liked the way it looked," Gasol said.

So he kept it.

"The beard gave Pau a change of attitude," Griz center Lorenzen Wright said. "It makes him look tougher. People don't know he's a little pussycat away from the court. They think he's a tiger."

The beard appeared to suddenly give Gasol newfound respect from referees.

"I look a little bit like a 10-year veteran now," Gasol said. "Some refs tell me I need to shave it, that it's way too long. Some say it really looks good. I don't know if they are telling the truth, but I've had a good year with it, and I feel comfortable with it."

3

BEYOND THE LOCKER-ROOM DOOR

NEED ANY EXTRA SALT?

Antonio Burks thought he had slipped under the radar during his rookie season in 2004-05. The point guard from the University of Memphis didn't believe that his rookie hazing would go beyond getting donuts for the team—or carrying veteran Lorenzen Wright's bags filled with a computer and DVDs on road trips. Burks had been very careful until the day he left his truck keys in a coat in his locker. And that's all the opening that then-Griz guard Bonzi Wells needed. "He was the brave one, but there was a gang of them," Burks said. Burks walked to his truck and discovered his entire front seat and half of his back seat had been filled with popcorn—not just sprinkled on the seat, but filled to the windowsill.

Welcome to the world of the NBA, Rook.

"I'm going to get them back," Burks vowed.

That may not be wise. Unless you're a protected rookie—meaning a certain veteran likes you so much he won't let other veterans pick on you—a rookie can expect to do whatever a veteran asks.

Bring donuts. Put the daily newspaper in the vet's locker. Carry a vet's bags on road trips whenever required.

"Everybody got me when I was rookie," said Wright, who spent his rookie season in 1996-97 with the Clippers. "My name was 'Rook' the whole season. They never even used my freakin' name. I wasn't called Lorenzen once my whole rookie year. I had to get out of the plane one time when it was snowing and help take bags off the plane and put them on the bus. I had bags of my own, and I'd have two or three people's bags."

So how did Wright survive it?

"The veterans would take you out and pay for your dinner," he said. "If you mess with the rookies a bit, you've got to reward them, too. I don't mess with them bad, as long as they do the little stuff we ask them to do. But last year [in 2003-04], our rookies Dahntay Jones and Troy Bell were acting up. …"

"Someone got my keys and filled my car with popcorn all the way to the headrest," said Bell, shortly before being released by the Grizzlies prior to the 2004-05 season. "It was terrible—buttered popcorn all over my leather seats. I thought 'Ren was involved and maybe [James] Posey."

Well, James?

"I don't remember," said a laughing Posey, a swingman who spent two seasons with the Griz from 2003-05.

Posey recalled his own rookie hazing with the Nuggets in 1999-2000.

"They had a big, strong guy like Roy Rogers, and he and some others would hold me down in a cold tub full of ice for two minutes," Posey said. "Or I'd be taking a shower, and someone would throw a bucket of ice on me."

Posey wasn't as fortunate as then-Griz guards Earl Watson and Jason Williams. In their respective rookie seasons at Seattle and Sacramento, each had a veteran protector.

"I was the first rookie point guard they had that Gary Payton actually loved and respected," said Watson, a rookie with the Sonics in 2001-02. "Gary didn't have me do anything. He said, 'You're with me.' He had second-year guys getting him food. He loved me. He called me 'his little brother.' I didn't have to do anything.

As former Griz guard Antonio Burks discovered, sly former Griz swingman Bonzi Wells knew how to indoctrinate rookies. © *2004 NBA Entertainment. Photo by Joe Murphy*

"He respected the way I respected the game, my work ethic and how bad I really wanted to win."

Williams' rookie season was 1998-99—the year the NBA played an abbreviated season because of a strike lockout. His veteran was Chris Webber, and since J-Will had a penchant for delivering C-Webb the ball when and where he wanted it, all was good.

"But we had this one rookie, Ryan Robertson, who didn't want to bring donuts when the veterans asked him," Williams recalled. "So they got hard on him. They made him bring some every day. They didn't even have to ask him the second half of the season. He just brought them. Two dozen donuts a day adds up on a rookie's contract, especially for a second-round pick."

Bonzi Wells, an instigator of Griz rookie pranks, was the victim of a few himself as a rookie with the Trail Blazers in 1998-99.

"I did my share of getting *USA Today*s, coffee, donuts, anything they ever needed on the road," said Wells. "I don't care if its 3, 4 or 5 in the morning, I better get up and do it. And I did a lot of that. The trick of this rookie-hazing thing is to be organized—find out what everybody likes, make a list, and come prepared. The first week, they caught me. From then, I was prepared."

For a rookie, the best thing about hazing is it lasts just that first year. Then, if you stay in the league, a veteran can get payback on rookies the rest of his career—as did Wells, who admits he likes the popcorn trick that was sprung on Bell, Jones, and Burks the best.

"We rounded up all the popcorn they didn't use [in The Pyramid], opened up Dahntay's sunroof, and poured it in there," Wells said. "Dahntay says he can still smell popcorn when he turns on his air conditioner."

There is one other way for a rookie to avoid hazing. Become a starter immediately, as Shane Battier and Pau Gasol did for the Griz as rookies in 2001-02. Battier and Gasol earned All-Rookie first team, and Gasol was the league's Rookie of the Year.

"About the only thing I had to do was sing in front of team, some soul classics like 'Let's Get It On' and, 'Let's Stay Together'," Battier said. "And that was about it. They knew that Pau and I were going to play 40 minutes a night, so they left us alone."

STRO, MEET YOUR SON

Mario Holt has been Griz locker-room attendant and ball boy for several years. But the first time he was introduced to former Grizzlies forward Stromile Swift, Swift's mouth dropped.

Yusef Boyd, the Grizzlies equipment manager and assistant trainer, could barely keep a straight face making the introduction.

"I told Stro that a lady came by The Pyramid [the Grizzlies' first home court in Memphis], said this child was yours and he needs to see you," Boyd said. "Stro laughed it off. But then he saw Mario, his jaw dropped, and we all busted out laughing. Not only did they look alike, both Mario and Stro even wore the same shoe size."

BRACKETOLOGISTS AT WORK

The 2005 NCAA men's basketball tournament selection committee didn't consider the Grizzlies' Earl Watson and Andre Emmett in the equation when the 65-team tourney bracket was announced.

In a first-round NCAA tourney game, Watson's UCLA Bruins were scheduled to play Emmett's Texas Tech Red Raiders. And as fate would have it, Watson and Emmett's lockers were next to each other in FedExForum during the '04-'05 season before Watson signed as a free agent with the Nuggets, and Emmett was waived.

The smack talk was hot and heavy:

Emmett: "Earl, what about a side bet?"

Watson: "You don't want to bet me."

Emmett: "You don't want to bet *me*—bet whatever you want, Earl."

Watson: "When Texas Tech runs out on the court, they're gonna think they saw [former UCLA center] Lew Alcindor. They're gonna get nervous. The UCLA fight song will start. They'll think about our 11 national championships. They're going to swear Coach [John] Wooden is over there coaching."

In some ways, the Grizzlies' locker room is somewhat like any other office in America the week that the newly announced NCAA Tournament brackets dominate the conversation. Yet, it's a bit different in that many Grizzlies have played in the NCAA tourney. Seven of the '04-'05 Grizzlies—Watson, Emmett, Shane Battier and Dahntay Jones [Duke], Mike Miller and Jason Williams [Florida], Stromile Swift [LSU], and Ryan Humphrey [Oklahoma]—were pulling for their former college teams that were in the tournament field that week.

Battier and Miller, are two of Grizzlies who have played in a national championship game. They track college basketball with a passion. Battier, traded to Houston in 2006, always directed the Grizzlies' locker-room NCAA tourney bracket contest.

"Mike and I follow college basketball like it's our hobby," Battier said. "We're on the road so much, there's nothing better than to turn on a television game and follow big schools and small schools. Having been to the finals and won once, it's fun for me to predict who has what it takes and who can make a great run. A lot of pride is on the line [when filling out brackets]. If your team gets knocked out of the tournament early, you don't want to come to practice the next day."

For Griz players such as Battier, having played in the NCAA Tournament heightens the passion for picking a bracket.

"The [NBA] playoffs are great, but the NCAA tournament in March has such a different feel," Battier said. "NBA playoffs are marathons. At least after the first three games of a series you know there's a tomorrow. In March Madness if you have one off-shooting night or your stud fouls out you're going to be watching the rest of the tournament at home."

Griz center and University of Memphis alum Lorenzen Wright agreed with Battier.

"Playing in the NCAA Tournament is one of the most exciting parts of your career," said Wright, who played in the '95 and '96 tournaments. "Everybody loves the tournament because that's when the last-second shots start to fall—from half-court, tip-ins, on drives. That's why they call it 'March Madness.'"

You don't have to tell Miller about that. ESPN picked its top 10 all-time tournament buzzer beaters, and included was Miller's game-winning drive to help No. 5 seed Florida edge 12th-seeded Butler, 69-68, in overtime of a first-round game in 2000.

His heroics started Florida on its march to the Final Four. Two games later Miller's Gators beat Battier's Dookies, 87-78, in an East Regional semifinal, then went on to lose in the national championship game to Michigan State, 89-76, before Miller decided to declare for the NBA draft.

"For sure that's [the basket against Butler] been the biggest shot of my career," Miller said. "If that shot doesn't go in, where does that leave me? I probably would've gone back to school [for his junior year].

"Then we beat Duke. Shane and I talk about that all the time. But he tells me he has a [national championship] ring [from '01] so I can't say much."

Battier, who played in four NCAA tournaments and two national championship games [losing, 77-74, to Connecticut in 1999 and beating Arizona 82-72 in '01], said he thanks Miller for the loss that ended Battier's junior year.

"I think before a champion can claim the throne they have to suffer some defeat," Battier said. "I firmly believe that, if we didn't lose that game to Florida, we wouldn't have been as strong and determined the next year to take the championship home. The year we won it we knocked out Maryland in the semifinals, and they came back the next year ['02] and won it."

So is that part of Battier's strategy when filling out his bracket? He won the Griz bracket competition his rookie season and finished third in '03-'04.

"I'm always pretty calculating," Battier said with laugh. "Since I've finished first and third, a lot of people are anxious to know what I do. But I can't divulge my strategy."

SPREADING THE WEALTH

If you grow up a gym rat, shooting basketball hours upon hours by yourself, naturally, your dream is to one day have a court in your backyard. Mike Miller was that kid in Mitchell, South Dakota. And now that Miller is a Grizzlies guard, taking home an NBA paycheck with a lot of zeroes on it, he's taken his dream to the next level.

"I've built a half-court gym right behind my house," said Miller, who also has had a couple of golf holes built on his extensive acreage at his Collierville home outside of Memphis. "Besides helping my parents retire, all I ever wanted was a gym."

For a three-point shooter like Miller, a home gymnasium—let's call it the Miller Fieldhouse—is a good investment.

"I think about so many horror stories of guys who go out and buy crazy things they never end up using," said former Grizzlies swingman Shane Battier, whose only initial splurge was buying one arcade-style video game. "Most players understand the value of a dollar a little bit better today because of the rookie programs that help you transition into the league. When you hear the horror stories, you tend to hold on to your money. At the same time, you want to enjoy it. Now that you have a very large disposable income, you can go out and buy something nice for you and your family."

Family is the recurring theme among the Grizzlies. They don't mind spending money on the ones they love.

"The main feeling I got by getting to the NBA was financial security for my family, myself, my brothers, sisters, and Mom," former Griz guard Earl Watson said, "and giving my little nieces and nephews better chances in education and location of residence. It was never like I wanted to play basketball to get this car or this house. It was more like, 'This is what I love to do, and it just so happens it pays a lot.' When I was younger, not too many people had multimillion-dollar deals, so you played basketball because you loved basketball. I just kept that same mind-set."

After taking care of his family, Watson said he has been conservative with his money, investing mostly in real estate.

"A lot of people try to get everything at once," Watson said. "But if you get everything at once, what else are you shooting for? You've got to place a goal, go get it, then place another goal and go get that. You have to take your time and enjoy life. You can't live your life in a short period of time, otherwise you won't enjoy anything."

Lorenzen Wright recalled how thrilling it was that he was able to surprise both his mother and grandmother by buying them new houses.

"I surprised my Mom with the new house," Wright said. "I had a limo come pick her up. She didn't know where she was going. I called her, told her, 'Just get in the limo.' The limo pulled up, we were there waiting at the new house and she said, 'What's this?' I said, 'This is your new house.' She started crying. Once I got her that new house, nothing else mattered to me."

Wright, who lives in Germantown halfway between his mother and grandmother's houses, also bought his grandmother a new car.

"When I bought my grandmother a car, she said it was the first time ever she'd had a new car," Wright said. "When we growing up, when we'd get a used car, we'd call it a new car. It was new to us. It was great to get my grandmother a car that was actually new. That meant a lot to me."

Former Grizzlies guard Jason Williams, traded to Miami before the 2005-06 season, also likes doting on his family.

"It makes me happy being able to buy things for my brother and my father and my grandmother, and seeing they are happy," Williams said. "I give my grandmother $400 a month, and you'd think she thinks it's $4 million because she can make $400 last two months. At some point in life, you've got to think, 'It's not about me; it's about my family now.' Being able to help people close to me makes me feel better than being able to go out buy a car or something for myself."

That's not to say each of the Grizzlies drives a wreck. With family as the first priority, the Griz players also have splurged a bit on themselves, buying nice rides ranging from Range Rovers to Hummers to Mercedes.

"When I first got in the league," said former Griz guard Bonzi Wells, "Walt Williams [a Portland teammate] had a Mercedes. That always intrigued me. I kept telling myself that I was going to get a Mercedes one day. I just wanted to drive that car and see that Mercedes emblem on the hood. It was the only thing I wanted.

"It took me a couple of years to save my money to get one. Finally, I got one. Just to have my own Mercedes, just to see that Mercedes emblem up front—knowing that I didn't steal it off anybody's car—means a lot."

SMALL IS COOL

Every NBA city can't be Los Angeles, New York, Chicago, Philadelphia, and other places where there are multiple major professional sports franchises. Sure there are some players who believe playing in one of the major media markets is vital to career advancement, who believe endorsements and exposure are greater in the big cities.

Yet there's also something to be said for being a one-horse pro town, such as an Orlando, a Salt Lake City, a Portland, and yes, a Memphis.

How much value can a player put on the less stressful lifestyle of playing and living in a small market? Or the lower cost of living? Or developing an intimate affair with the fans who love the only pro team in town?

"Sometimes you might like playing in big markets," said Grizzlies guard Mike Miller, who played for Orlando before being traded to the Grizzlies. "But I do like playing in a smaller city, because I'm comfortable in a smaller city. This city is great; the people are great; it reminds me of back home. It's easier when the outside life is easy and not as hectic and not as quick like the big city."

"The lifestyle is so laidback and easy compared to if you're playing in New York or Chicago. In those places, you're always going; it takes you at least at hour or more to get to work. This right here is such a great setting."

Former Griz point guard Jason Williams, another small-town product from Belle, West Virginia, agreed. "I'm from a town with 1,500 people, so every city is big to me," he said, who broke into the league with Sacramento. "At same time, I'd rather play in small market. Traffic is awful in larger cities, especially if you don't like to drive like myself."

Being the only pro team in a market is a huge advantage. Former Grizzlies point guard Earl Watson, who played collegiately at UCLA in Los Angeles, said larger cities have more diversions.

"Even when I played a game at UCLA, the Lakers or Clippers might play the same night as we played," said Watson. "If we played North Carolina, the place might be sold out. But otherwise, we suffered from it."

Watson is one of the few Grizzlies who previously played professionally in a large market.

"In a bigger market, you get more attention," Watson said. "It's like you're on the block to be chopped, with the media attacking you all the time. I loved it. It made my game rise to a whole other level. I had no problem playing under that pressure—it was fun. But it's also okay to be laidback. A lot of times people complicate life and complicate what they do. Here, I just have to play basketball, work hard to improve my game, do the best I can, try get better every week, and everything will fall in place. Exposure is better for personal business, but wherever you win, attention will come your way."

Grizzlies center Lorenzen Wright began his pro career in Los Angeles with the Clippers, and then went to the Hawks before returning to the city where he starred as a college player. There's no doubt coming home is his favorite place to play.

"Playing here is more like a family," Wright said. "Everybody is watching us; everybody is talking about us, no matter where you go. I haven't heard anybody say here that they don't like the Grizzlies. People in L.A. who hate the Lakers love the Clippers. When I played at other places, like in Atlanta, people would be like, 'I hate the Hawks; they don't ever win.' You have a whole lot of people who don't like the team. But here, everybody loves the Grizzlies."

It certainly doesn't hurt that Memphis' long-time reputation as a basketball town makes it an attractive place to play.

"The people are really great here, they understand the game of basketball because it's a basketball city," said Mike Miller. "But they are also regular people who treat you like regular people, which is phenomenal."

Griz forward Shane Battier, who was with the team from the time it moved to Memphis from Vancouver in 2001 through the 2005-06 season, said the city has adapted to the Griz.

"Initially, people didn't know how to act if they saw one of us in public," Battier said. "At first, people would go ballistic if they saw a Grizzly, because they couldn't believe we were at a supermarket. There were some people who didn't know what to say. I think people now understand we're normal Memphians—we go to the grocery store, we go to the movies."

Battier particularly enjoyed the relationships he developed with fans.

"I like it from the standpoint that I've become familiar with faces," Battier said in 2005. "I know who Mark Goodfellow [a used-car dealer] is; I know guys who have front-row tickets. And I know a lot of families that come to autograph events. I don't think you get that in bigger cities. I think that's cool that I can see someone in the street and know who they are."

For some players, a move to a smaller city may be what the doctor ordered. Such was the case with Bonzi Wells.

In Portland, Wells, Rasheed Wallace, and others got a reputation as being malcontents. The trade to Memphis rejuvenated Wells' basketball career, before a coaching change from Hubie Brown to Mike Fratello early in the 2004-05 season soured Wells on his situation. He was traded before the '05-'06 season to Sacramento.

Still, that didn't mean Wells didn't enjoy playing in a small market.

"In Portland, you had to stay at a high level or they'd boo you, or write negative stuff," Wells said. "But here, the Southern hospitality is so beautiful, so real and so respectful."

Wells had no problem with the city, just with Fratello, which is why he was sent packing. But for at least one and a half seasons, he found tranquility on and off the court in Memphis.

THROWIN' BACK THE THROWBACKS

Back before the '04-'05 season, when the NBA instituted a dress code that required a fashion sense from its players, an NBA locker room looked like a store for throwback jerseys from all pro sports. NBA players couldn't get enough of them, and the Grizzlies were no different.

"You want to walk in wearing the throwback jersey that nobody has," said former Griz forward James Posey. "You want that throwback that's not even on the market."

The Griz player who had the most throwbacks was Stromile Swift, who possessed more than 50 in his closet. He had everything from old-school NBA stars to former NFL stars Barry Sanders and Steve Largent, to former Major Leaguers such as Pete Rose.

"You can get just about any jersey custom made if you know what it looked like," Swift said. "You could probably get a Shane Battier high school jersey made."

Former Griz guard Jason Williams said he didn't even have to like the player to buy the guy's throwback jersey—"For instance, I have a Bill Walton throwback," he said.

Earl Watson, another former Grizzly, was big on getting jerseys that linked him to his childhood of growing up in Kansas City.

"I had a Kansas City Royals baby blue throwback," Watson said. "I also wear a lot of jerseys as a sign of respect for the way that guy played, like a UCLA Alcindor [Kareem Abdul-Jabbar] jersey, and a Jerry West college throwback from his West Virginia days."

Griz guard Mike Miller leaned toward his heroes, Larry Bird and Pete Maravich, but also has several Negro League throwbacks because "nobody else on our team has them."

Lorenzen Wright's prized items are USC and Buffalo Bills jerseys of running back O.J. Simpson.

"I wear O.J. … he's innocent," said Wright defending his jersey choice. "They said he was innocent, so he was innocent."

There were nights, though, in the Grizzlies' locker room when a couple of players wore the same throwback.

"Happened to me three times in one season with Jason," Wright said. "It got to where we talked to each other to coordinate what we were going to wear."

Former Griz coach Hubie Brown found the throwback fad amusing since he coached many of the players in the '70s and '80s who have been immortalized in throwback jerseys.

"What's really nice is that the jerseys remember a great player that some of our younger guys may not be familiar with," Brown said. "When I see one of guys wearing a throwback, I ask them, 'Do you know who this player is and what he did?'"

FLYING FIRST CLASS

It's a world of travel that the average Joe never gets to see—riding high on a private NBA team plane. The Grizzlies are no different. They travel on a modified 727, where there are three compartments with 56 deluxe leather seats.

The front compartment is for the players, featuring 16 oversized seats and a table for watching DVDs. The middle compartment is for the coaching staff and has 12 seats and two VCRs for watching game tape. The rear compartment has 28 seats for support personnel.

A typical road trip starts like this:

A player drives his cars to a private hangar at the Memphis airport— all the way up to the rear steps of the plane where one attendant grabs his bags and another parks his car. As he boards the plane, a stewardess greets a player saying, "Would you like some fajitas before we take off?" Once in the air, he has a meal choice of steak or blackened catfish, then desserts of ice cream bars and freshly baked chocolate-chip cookies.

When the team returns to Memphis from a trip and they step off the plane, their cars are already on the runway, with the engines running and trunks open waiting for luggage.

"It's so nice that I hardly want to travel in the off-season knowing that I've got to go through lines in airports and check bags," Shane Battier said. "It's enough to make me want to stay home."

4

THE DOOKIE

DRAFT-DAY DECISIONS

T hen-Grizzlies Director of Basketball Operations Dick Versace said it was tough parting with veteran Griz forward Shareef Abdur-Rahim in the 2001 draft-day trade.

"We decided that, if Shareef was our best player, we were going to have a tough time, because we didn't have more assets than just him," Versace said. "We worked a long time on the Shareef trade. He was a coveted player. It was hard personally to trade him because you're talking about one of the greatest human beings you'll ever meet. But we needed more assets on this club. You have to look what we got from the trade—we got Lorenzen Wright and Pau Gasol, and that's two starters for one."

When the Grizzlies moved up in the draft, they had one last decision.

"The biggest decision was what do we do if we're faced with taking Tyson Chandler or Pau," Versace said. "I'd been studying the tapes of Pau, and we sent many people to watch Pau over the last two years, including [general manager] Billy Knight and [then-scouting director] Tony [Barone]. We wanted Pau."

The Grizzlies had a picking order in mind for the No. 6 spot overall. They would go for Jason Richardson, if available, then Shane Battier, and then Richard Jefferson if Richardson and Battier had been taken.

"Everything fell the way we wanted," Versace said. "We were looking to get character on the ballclub at that time because it was desperately needed, and Shane was our choice there. We had calculated that Shane would be there."

Battier, college basketball's Player of the Year for national champion Duke, was smooth when he put on a Griz cap on draft night.

"Hey, FedEx is the best shipping company in the world," said Battier, giving a nod to the Memphis-based shipping company. "I'm so thrilled to be playing for the Grizzlies. I was very impressed with my interviews with them."

Battier admitted he was jittery before the draft.

"It was probably the most nervous day of my life, I really didn't enjoy the day," Battier recalled. "I had every scenario on my mind. I walked around New York with my head in the clouds thinking of different possibilities. I gave Memphis a thought for a second, but I didn't know anything about the city or the franchise enough to visualize myself there. When I was chosen, when they called my name, I closed my eyes. I was just happy I was going to have an address. I was homeless. I'd just been kicked out of my college dorm. I was relieved that I could take my car, drive to a new city, and have a home. To be honest with you, it could have been Alaska, and I would have been happy."

Knight was thrilled to get Battier.

"You like to add a guy with charm, intelligence, and good looks, but you also like to get a guy who is a player, too," Knight said. "We got a guy who can help be the foundation of this team."

Battier said he wasn't going to get carried away with the sudden wealth attached to a first-round draft choice.

"The biggest thing I've purchased so far has been new golf balls," he said. "I bought a lot, $80 worth, because I'm not very good. I'm not good enough to get the Tour Precision balls. Those are too high-quality for me. I get the rocks."

No Grizzly player connected as strongly with the Memphis community as Shane Battier. © 2006 NBA Entertainment. Photo by Joe Murphy

And in a bit of irony, the Grizzlies' draft was assessed on draft night by TNT analyst Hubie Brown who said, "The Grizzlies have had a nice little draft."

GARDEN PARTY

As a player at Duke, Shane Battier had played in New York's fabled Madison Square Garden six times. His seventh trip, his first as an NBA player, was a lot of fun. Off a designed play, Battier hit a game-winning baseline jumper with 9.8 seconds left to give the Griz a 90-88 win.

"This is what big-time NBA basketball is all about. the Garden is a special place to play," said Battier, who scored 21 points. "I was shocked to see how open I was. I was expecting to see [Latrell] Sprewell or Allan Houston fly at me, but I had a good look."

Griz Coach Sidney Lowe didn't hesitate designing the game-winning shot for his rookie.

"He's accustomed to being in these positions," Lowe said. "That's why I designed the play for him to get the ball in his hands."

BATTIER, HUBIE, AND COACH K

Shane Battier has been fortunate to be managed by two of the greatest coaches in the game—first in college under Mike Krzyzewski at Duke and then by Hubie Brown with the Griz.

"Coach K is play-with-your-heart guy," Battier said. "Hubie believes with playing with your heart, but he's also a stats guy. Hubie has been around a while. He has a system where you try to get a certain number of deflections, a certain number of fast breaks, certain number of scoring opportunities on the offensive boards. I don't know how many coaches talk about that. I haven't been around coaches who emphasize those three things."

LAST-SECOND SHANE

Ever since being part of the two-man foundation drafted by the Grizzlies in '01 along with Gasol, Battier has had a knack for making plays in the clutch. Given his basketball education in the Duke program, it's a given that he knows how to win games.

On February 8, 2004, at Minnesota in a 99-98 victory, the Grizzlies were trailing by a point with 15 seconds left when Hubie Brown sent Battier into the game for Bo Outlaw.

"The reason we went with Battier at the end was because we knew we needed another scorer on the floor," Brown said. "We didn't want to go to Pau against [Kevin] Garnett. Shane had a smaller guy on him, and he's a clutch shooter."

The final play took a while to develop, but point guard Jason Williams got the ball to Battier, who drove toward the right baseline. He had defender Sam Cassell beat by a step, and Battier stunned Cassell by pulling up and hitting the game-winning jumper with 2.8 seconds left.

"We ran a pick and roll with Jason, they switched up; and Jason made a good pass to get it to me," Battier said. "It took a long time for the play to develop, and I was worried we weren't going to get a good shot. So I just took two hard dribbles and let it fly."

BEATING THE HOMEBOYS

On Shane Battier's list of things to do, it took him four seasons to check off "beat my homeboys from Detroit."

Battier calmly sank four free throws in the final 20 seconds, being fouled on a loose-ball scramble and on a rebound, to boost the Griz to a 72-68 victory over the defending NBA champion Pistons early in the '04-'05 season.

"I can go home now—this is the only team I haven't beaten in this league," said Battier, born in the Detroit suburb of Birmingham and who starred in high school at Detroit Country Day. "It's nice I can go back now and not get the catcalls from my family and friends."

DID SOMEONE GET A PICTURE OF THAT?

Battier stormed toward the basket, flipped a switch on the jet engines in his sneakers, and threw down an impressive dunk over Portland shot-blocker Joel Pryzbilla in a 104-83 late season win in '04-'05.

"That was a Haley's Comet dunk," Battier said with a sly smile. "You won't see it again the rest of this century. I hope you didn't blink because it won't happen again. Really, I don't know who has those kind of rocket boosters at this point of the season."

SIMPLY EN FUEGO

In the back of Battier's locker during the '04-'05 season was a small piece of paper given to him by fan. On the paper was a quote from philosopher Ralph Waldo Emerson that Battier particularly liked. It said, "What lies behind us and what lies before us are tiny matters compared to what lies within us."

That might be a bit deep for the average NBA player, but Battier isn't the average NBA player. His jump shot is as deep as his Duke education, which stuns some teams, as when he hit a career-high 33 against Toronto in an 86-75 victory in the '04-'05 season.

The sizzling Battier was so ridiculous in that game, it seemed like everyone of his shots deserved style points—whether he was shooting a baseline fall-away over an aggravated Jalen Rose or a stumbling drive for a three-point play to beat the shot clock.

Pau Gasol, Shane Battier, and then-Griz coach Sidney Lowe hug after the team's first regular-season victory ever in Memphis in '01-'02.
© 2001 NBA Entertainment. Photo by Joe Murphy

But the shot that rocked the house and got the entire Griz bench on its feet—the dagger that gave the Grizzlies a 10-point lead and forced the Raptors to call a timeout with 1:27 left—was a falling out-of-bounds, deep-left corner three-pointer as the shot clock expired.

Even Battier was forced to smile over that one. At that point, he knew just about anything he threw up was going to fall.

"I read a lot of philosophy books, and they talk about a zone where you don't think about what you're doing," said Battier, who hit 10-of-17 field goals, including 4-of-5 from beyond the arc, and 9-of-11 free throws. "You just act, it sort of happens; you don't really remember it."

Said Griz center Lorenzen Wright, "When Shane hit that last three— standing on his tippy toes, falling out-of-bounds, throwing it up and it goes in—you can't teach that."

Battier abused 6-foot-8 Raptors swingman Rose so badly in the post, that Toronto put 6-foot-10 Chris Bosh on Battier. Rose got so miffed that he got a technical foul in the final minute and then was ejected from the game for a flagrant foul committed against Earl Watson. Rose took off his jersey and threw it in the stands as he exited the court.

"I don't know how I hit some of those shots in the second half," Battier said. "Sometimes it doesn't look very pretty, but at the end of the day, I'll take them. It's rare you feel like that in sports. You have weeks you are on fire and weeks that you might be horrible."

SHANE THE VILLAIN

It had been a while since Battier had played the role of the villain. But Battier became the bad guy, at least in the eyes of the Suns' fans during game one of the '05 playoffs, when he sent Phoenix's Shawn Marion to the floor with a physical foul with 8:29 left in the third quarter.

Battier and Stromile Swift hit Marion as he drove to the basket trying to cash in a steal. Battier whacked Marion on his shooting arm, and Marion fell to the floor landing on his right wrist.

Marion stayed down for several minutes before getting up, going to the foul line, making the second of two free throws. Battier was a bit surprised that the foul was ruled flagrant, and Marion said afterward he didn't believe the foul was intentional. "Battier's not that type of player," Marion emphasized.

"I don't want to say anything that will cost me money," said Battier, carefully choosing his words so the league wouldn't fine him for criticizing officiating. "The way I look at it, if the roles were reversed and I had an easy lay-up, I'd be on the ground, too. That's playoff basketball. I wasn't trying to hurt him [Marion]. I was trying to stop a lay-up, we got tangled up; and he went down."

For the rest of the game after Marion got hurt, Phoenix fans booed Battier every time he touched the ball. It reminded him of his college days at Duke, where every stop on the Atlantic Coast Conference trail was more hostile than the next.

"Maryland was much worse than Phoenix," Battier said with a laugh. "At Maryland, I had batteries and ice thrown at me, I was spit on, people cursed me out. It was much worse than this."

IT'S HIS CITY

Battier tries to view the NBA as a business.

"I'm an employee of the NBA, and I happen to work for the Memphis branch," he said before being traded to Houston in June 2006. "But I love it here. My wife loves it here. We feel like Memphians. When I step away from basketball, I'm just normal Shane, a goofy guy who wants to do good by other people and use what I have to help others. But when I come to the office, I do the best I can at the office."

JUST A BALLER

During the course of his Grizzlies career, Battier played four positions and even developed a solid post offense complete with jump hooks from either hand. He thrived on the challenge of guarding Kobe Bryant or Tracy McGrady or Vince Carter on the perimeter on one night, then having to belly up inside against Elton Brand or Kevin Garnett.

"Most people are at a desk all week working on the same project," Battier said. "I'm lucky in that I get to take on a new project every week, almost every game."

So how can he go from tailing a Kobe to an Elton Brand?

"I know I'm not 250 pounds—I know I can't bang with big guys," Battier said. "So I have to know the plays, pay attention to the scouting report, learn every angle I can. Then, I've got to go out and physically battle someone. It's all about being basketball players—forget titles and positions—and understanding how to play the game. It's being in the right position at the right time. You're not going to be perfect doing that, but you're going to be successful for a long period of time."

Every coach who ever coached Battier falls in love with his basketball I.Q. and his perspective on life.

"He's an unbelievable member of a team whether he starts or subs," Griz Coach Mike Fratello said. "He knows what he can and can't do; and he doesn't play outside of what he can do."

TIME'S UP

Battier, absolutely one of the best players in the NBA dealing with the media, would stay all night after a game answering questions. He's that nice of a guy, and his wife, Heidi, knows it.

So tired of her husband being the last player out of the locker room, Battier heeded to his wife's wishes for the '05-'06 season. He placed a timer in his locker and set it at 15 minutes—the time it takes to ice his knees and ankles sitting at his locker after a game. When the buzzer sounds, interviews and icing is over.

"I'm trying to be a better, efficient husband," Battier said.

MAGICAL ADVICE

One of Battier's strengths is his constant desire to learn and improve. It's something that should give him a 15-year NBA career if his body holds up.

"I heard Magic Johnson speak at a lot of camps when I was younger," Battier said. "He said to try and add something to your game every summer. Focus on one part of your game and expand it. That's what I've done since I was 10 or 11 years old."

ONCE A WINNER, ALWAYS A WINNER

Battier has seen both ends of the spectrum in his basketball career. He came from a perennial collegiate power in Duke, where he twice played in the Final Four and won the national championship in 2001 when he was the Player of the Year. Then he ended up with the Grizzlies, maybe the worst franchise in the NBA when he was drafted.

Yet through it all, he has maintained his perspective.

"I was drafted [by Memphis] to help grow the foundation of a pro basketball culture in this city," said Battier during the '05-'06 season. "To make the playoffs two years in a row is unbelievable, and it's great that I had a role in it. It's much different than trying to maintain a championship level [like at Duke]. It's a tougher challenge in many regards. You have to taste adversity to appreciate success."

Battier remembers his rookie year as being one of survival.

"As a rookie, I didn't know any better," Battier said. "I was just trying to go out and play with fire. I look at film of my rookie year, I had more hair and more spring, but I wouldn't trade it for the veteran savvy I have now."

THE OLYMPIC INVITE

Seeking the right chemistry for the 2008 Olympic team, Battier got an invite in March '06 to try out for the U.S. team. He was thrilled, and his teammates were happy for him.

"Obviously, it's an honor to be mentioned in the same breath of the all stars in this league," Battier said. "It's a pivotal time for USA Basketball. They've taken a lot of shots from people over the past few years, and it's time to assemble a team to reclaim its rightful crown."

HEADS UP

On three occasions during the '05-'06 season, Battier had his head split by an opposing player's elbow. The second time happened against the Bulls, just before Christmas.

"I don't know what it is," Battier said of getting whacked again. "I'm a good citizen. I donate blood to the Red Cross. It's the holiday season, but I think they got the wrong idea about giving. Some things, like stitches, you just don't give."

SO LONG, CITIZEN SHANE

On draft night 2006, it seemed as if Memphis became a legitimate NBA franchise. Griz President Jerry West did the unthinkable. He traded Battier, the team's biggest fan favorite on and off the floor, to the Houston Rockets, for the draft rights to University of Connecticut-rookie Rudy Gay and former Griz Stromile Swift.

Battier got the news while eating dinner with some of the people who worked his summer basketball camp. He took the call, came back to the table, and announced, "I've just been traded." Then he carried on with dinner as if nothing had happened. It wasn't until a day or two later, when his camp was ending and he was giving one last speech to the campers, that he got a bit emotional.

Much of Memphis got emotional with him. *The Commercial Appeal* was flooded with letters and emails from admiring Battier fans. Some were hurt that he was traded. Others thanked him profusely for being a shining example of a team player who played clean and hard.

"I never set out to be the guy on the billboards or the guy in the commercials," Battier told Ron Tillery of *The Commercial Appeal*. "Through circumstances, it came to be that way. I was proud to don a Memphis jersey and be that guy people could look to for a pulse of the Griz."

Though Battier played for one of college basketball's best programs at Duke, he never lost sight of the growth progress of the Grizzlies franchise. His words moments after the Grizzlies were swept from the playoffs by the Mavs in April 2006 ring true, even after his departure:

"You pick yourself back up. What fun is life if you don't have challenges that you can't overcome? There's no sense in wilting now and giving it up for loss. You pick yourself back up, you get to work this summer, and you try to get better. That's what this journey is all about."

5

WERE YOU THERE THE NIGHT THAT...

WELCOME TO MEMPHIS

U sually in Memphis, an early October event means a big college football game is in the offing. But on October 9, 2001, when the Grizzlies finally hit the court for the first time in a 99-95 exhibition victory over the Portland Trail Blazers, the 14,250 fans in The Pyramid rocked the house.

Technically, the game didn't count—but it surely mattered, and every Grizzly knew that. That's why they came from 18 down in the first half to win the game.

"The whole city wanted to win it," said Griz rookie forward Shane Battier. "You could feel the 25 years of anxiety in one evening."

Hometown product Lorenzen Wright, who had 13 points and 13 rebounds, said it had been a long time since he had heard a crowd that loud.

"We wanted to show the crowd what we could do," Wright said. "This isn't the Vancouver Grizzlies. We wanted to shake that bad reputation."

Over in the visitors' locker room, Portland guard Damon Stoudamire understood the reaction of the Grizzlies' fans.

"I've been through something like this before, because I was in Toronto the first year," Stoudamire said. "Here, it's like being an expansion team all over again, because they are trying to win over the fans. I'd say they won over the fans."

OPENING NIGHT

They trotted out the big guns for the first regular-season NBA game in Memphis history on November 1, 2001. There were Memphians Isaac Hayes and Justin Timberlake singing "God Bless America" and the national anthem respectively.

There was NBA commissioner David Stern telling the crowd, "Good evening, and welcome to NBA basketball, Memphis."

And there was a 90-80 loss to the Pistons. Blame the loss on a couple of downtown Memphis restaurants, the Rendezvous and Melanie's. It's where Pistons star Jerry Stackhouse ate on his first trip to Memphis, and it must have agreed with him—he scored 34 points.

"I'm sorry we've got to come here just one time this year, because the food is something else around here," Stackhouse said.

SO THIS IS WHAT A WIN FEELS LIKE

Eight straight Griz losses to open the first season had Griz fans and players tense about when the team would finally break through to the win column. It finally happened with a 98-93 victory over the Cavaliers on November 17, 2001, in The Pyramid. The Griz made sure it happened by shooting 64 percent in the fourth quarter thanks to the steady hand of Jason Williams, who finished with 16 points and 14 assists.

The Grizzlies came from 13 points down in the third quarter, even making the run to victory without center Lorenzen Wright, who left the game in the third with neck and back spasms.

"One [win] looks a lot better than zero," said rookie Shane Battier after scoring 20 points to lead the Griz.

TAPS FOR SIDNEY ON A TUBA

Sidney Lowe's final game as the Grizzlies' head coach—an 108-101 loss to Golden State to doom the Griz to an 0-8 start to the '02-'03 season—had an unusual twist.

Prior to the game, Geoff Calkins, columnist for *The Commercial Appeal* in Memphis, wrote that he would play his tuba outside The Pyramid the next home game if the Grizzlies didn't beat the Warriors. He guaranteed a victory.

When the Warriors walked into their locker room before the game, copies of Calkins' column graced every locker.

"Can that guy really play the tuba?" asked Warriors forward Antawn Jamison.

As luck (or fortunate scheduling) would have it, Calkins wasn't at the game. But that didn't stop Jamison from stopping by press row late in the game and saying, "Where's that guy with the tuba? He'd better be warming up."

The next day, Lowe was fired, and Hubie Brown replaced him.

GETTING THE GOAT

Desperate times call for desperate measures. So when the Grizzlies, even after hiring Hubie Brown early in the '02-'03 season, saw their losing streak extend to 0-13 to open the year, it was time for Beale Street bar owner Silky O'Sullivan to step in.

O'Sullivan took his lucky goat, Maynard the Magnificent, over to The Pyramid, where Maynard circled the statue of Ramses, and shamrocks were sprinkled to remove the hex of losing. O'Sullivan claimed it was an Irish custom to use a goat to break the hex, which he said was the result of angry pharaohs.

"They're not happy because the Grizzlies are moving out of the building in a couple of years [to the FedExForum]," Sullivan said at the time.

A night later, the Grizzlies beat Washington for their first win, then beat Seattle before losing to the NBA champion Lakers in overtime.

"It's the power of the goat," O'Sullivan said. "It's the power of the goat."

HEY BUDDY

It's no secret that some of the toughest fans in the NBA are in Philadelphia. During a Griz game in the '03-'04 season, a Philly fan behind the Griz bench verbally rode Shane Battier, which was quite amazing, since Battier is one of the most poised players in the league.

Finally, then-Griz coach Hubie Brown's New Jersey roots came to the forefront.

He turned to general direction of the loudmouth and said, "Hey! Whoever's yelling: You should hope to Christ that you have a son like this in your life. This kid's legit, okay? He's the best. That's what you should know."

The guy shut up.

Hubie 1, 76ers crowd 0.

DON'T PUNK POSEY

Former Griz James Posey had many great moments in '03-'04, which was his first season in Memphis. But in a loss at Sacramento on December 23, he did something that told to the rest of the league what the Grizzlies of 2003-04 were going to be.

In the final seconds of the game, Kings forward Peja Stojakovic had 38 points and needed two more for a career high. Instead of running out the clock, Stojakovic decided to drive to the basket to get two more points. Posey, incensed by the move, simply grabbed Stojakovic and threw him to the floor. The play earned Posey an ejection with 11 seconds left, but it also earned the respect of his teammates.

While some of the Kings' players, such as Vlade Divac, were aghast over Posey's move—"The guy that threw him down should focus on playing defense in the first quarter"—Posey had no regrets about what he did.

"What he [Stojakovic] was trying to do wasn't necessary, because they already had the game," Posey said. "I just wasn't having it. What I did probably would have been more vicious back in the day."

When Stojakovic played his next game in Memphis just more than a month after the throw-down with Posey, the Grizzlies' crowd booed every time Stojakovic touched the ball. He was held to just 11 points and no three-pointers in a 109-95 Griz win.

"We didn't forget about that [first] game, and neither did our fans," Posey said of the home-crowd support. "A few thousand people expressing their opinion rattled him a bit."

THE MOTHER OF ALL DUNKS

If it were up to former Griz forward Stromile Swift, he'd prefer to remember the turning point of his '03-'04 season when he scored in double figures six straight games in March.

"But I know the fans like to talk about that dunk, that's one of the most exciting highlights of the year," Swift said.

Swift, a fearless dunker with a 40-inch-plus vertical, had a dunk almost every game that could qualify for *SportsCenter* highlights. But his dunk just before time ran out on a December 13, 2003, blowout of the Nets in The Pyramid will be shown long after he retires.

Former Griz guard Bonzi Wells and Swift were together on a breakaway when Wells threw a lob pass that seemed too high and leaning away from the goal. When Swift went airborne, reached back with one hand toward the roof, palmed the ball, and stuffed the ball through the basket in one sweeping motion. Even he was so amazed that he threw his head back and started howling once he landed.

NIGHT OF THE TECHNICALS

There were so many whistles, you'd thought a supermodel was styling and profiling at mid-court. In a 99-92 loss to the Warriors on February 25, 2004, the Grizzlies got hit with a team-record five technical fouls. Griz coach Hubie Brown was excused midway through the fourth quarter, drawing his second technical foul and the automatic ejection.

"I'm really pissed," Brown said afterwards.

Memphis led 57-54 when referee Joey Crawford's attempt to establish order backfired. Crawford warned Brown, Warriors coach Eric Musselman, and their teams to stop complaining or risk ejection. But it wasn't long after Crawford delivered the message that the officials completely lost control.

Cha-ching! High-flying Griz forward Stromile Swift cashes in a dunk over Houston's Yao Ming. © 2005 NBA Entertainment. Photo by Joe Murphy

Bonzi Wells received an offensive foul on an 18-foot jump shot. But the replay showed that Warriors guard Jason Richardson got hit by incidental contact as Wells elevated for his shot.

Wells turned to Crawford and spread his arms in amazement, which earned him a technical foul. The Griz were tagged with a defensive three-seconds call moments later. Then, referee Tim Donaghy hit Lorenzen Wright with a 'T'. The tension escalated as Crawford almost instantaneously hit Wright with another 'T' before changing the call and tagging James Posey instead.

"It was strange, a weird game," Griz forward Pau Gasol said. "I guess the referees got tired of everything to the point when you couldn't say anything in a quiet or in a normal way, or just to get some advice. You couldn't even put your hands up. They called technical [fouls] mostly against us; and it breaks your momentum."

Golden State received just one technical foul, to Calbert Cheaney after he used profanity to argue a call in the second period. The technical fouls directed toward the Griz were bizarre—from the one that got Brown ejected, to Wright receiving two for apparently trying to fire up his teammates, to Wright having one of those technicals pawned off on Posey because it would have meant an ejection for Wright.

"I've never seen anything like this in my life," Wright said. "I'm not saying any names, but I heard people talk about how they don't like Hubie before the game. But we just have to keep playing hard and get this game back."

Brown said he didn't have a negative history with Crawford. But the longtime official clearly worked the game with a combative attitude. Just before the outbreak of technicals, Crawford warned both teams to shut their mouths. "Tell your guys to stop [complaining] because I'm going to start to dump people," Crawford told Brown and Musselman.

Crawford eventually tossed Brown with 6:14 left in the fourth quarter. Brown's crime?

"He went over the back," Brown yelled, complaining that Warriors center Erick Dampier committed a foul while scoring a tip-in over Wright's head.

"I've had enough of you," Crawford responded, "Get out of here."

Then-Griz coach Hubie Brown takes a walk after being ejected by the officials.
© 2004 NBA Entertainment. Photo by Joe Murphy

Grizzlies majority owner Michael Heisley, who was in the house, wasn't happy.

"I thought the game got completely out of control. There were excessive fouls called, and the number of technicals was ludicrous," Heisley said. "It was almost like a meltdown of the officiating. I was sorry to see it. I was somewhat shocked. I know you're going to have bad calls and you live with it. But to see the people of Memphis so upset, it made me feel bad. I didn't think it was in the best interest of the NBA. That game didn't help sell pro basketball in Memphis. I was saddened by it more than angered by it because I'm an owner in the league. It's a partnership. In effect, what hurts the league hurts me. I'm thinking, 'Oh, my God. Are some of these people not coming back?'

"I wouldn't think that Joey Crawford came in there with something against the Grizzlies," Heisley added. "I think he got upset about something. I don't know if it was something outside of the game or what. He got upset and took over the game. The officials were definitely the most visible people on the floor. That was definitely regrettable. I don't know if the league wants that to happen."

A GAME IS JUST A GAME

There are times when sports takes a back seat to real life, such as the case on March 19, 2003, when President Bush announced the United States and its allies were going to war with Iraq.

The announcement came with 2:49 left to play in what was to become a 128-101 Griz win over the Cavaliers. Griz guard Jason Williams had just dribbled the ball across half-court when the horn blew, stopping play. By jaw-dropping coincidence, the time of night was 9:11 CST.

Players from both teams went to the locker rooms, watching Bush announce on television, "We will accept no outcome but victory." The crowd of 12,506 in the Pyramid, viewing the announcement on the scoreboard, responded with a partial standing ovation. After a 15-minute delay, the game resumed and quietly ended. Afterward, Griz swingman Shane Battier put the night in perfect perspective.

"A lot of us have friends in the military in that region, and we all want this conflict solved as quickly as possible," Battier said. "But I know we all have a role to play in this world. Many times, people scoff at our profession and those in the entertainment industry. But we know there are so many people in this country who work hard and who are under pressure who need to take a break from the world events. That's when they can watch sports on TV, or maybe come to a Grizzlies game and relax for a few hours.

"I was watching *SportsCenter* and it was pretty moving to me when they were talking to a young infantry man in Kuwait," Battier continued. "He was saying how sports were to our guys and gals in the Middle East. A lot of them follow us and want us to keep on keeping on. So my approach is I'm going to do my job as an American. I'm going to do my job to the best of my ability, and try to bring a piece of America to the Middle East, and raise morale over there."

BUT, BUT, BUT ... COACH!

Young players many times play with one eye on the action and one eye looking at their head coach. In an exhibition game in 2004 against the Hawks, second-year guard Troy Bell was trying hard to please Hubie Brown. So when Bell had an open shot late in the game, he remembered Brown screaming at him the day before in practice not to take the shot, to keep running the offense.

But in this case, versus the Hawks, Brown told Bell, "You've got to shoot the ball when you're open!"

Bell looked at Brown with a confused expression and said, "Yesterday, in practice, you yelled at me for shooting that shot."

The entire Grizzlies bench began laughing and even Brown had to smile.

It wasn't the first time Bell had been baffled by Brown's instructions. When Bell came to Memphis for a summer pre-draft workout, along with future Griz teammate Dahntay Jones of Duke and Dwyane Wade of Marquette, it wasn't like any other workout they'd attended.

"Hubie flipped out on us, screaming at us and telling us we weren't working hard," Bell said with a laugh. "I didn't even know he was the coach. All I knew about the Grizzlies was Jerry West."

THIS IS NOT A DREAM

Mike Golub, the Grizzlies' vice-president of business operations, still couldn't quite believe the Griz had made the '03-'04 playoffs, even as he stood at gate A14 of Memphis International Airport to board a Northwest jet bound for San Antonio and the first game of the first-round Western Conference series.

"This is weird," Golub said. "I'm getting on a plane to go to a playoff game, and it's actually my own team."

IT'S HARD NOT TO REMEMBER THE ALAMO

Grizzlies' radio analyst Sean Tuohy had the best description of the noise level in the Spurs' SBC Center for the Grizzlies' opening two games of a best-of-seven Western Conference series in '03-'04.

"It's like Elvis entered the building and never left," Tuohy said.

Griz forward Shane Battier noticed the noise level in SBC Center during game one.

"It was great," he said. "I'm used to it, because it was like when I played at Duke. I like it loud."

Grizzlies coach Hubie Brown said, while crowd noise is different at various arenas because of the building configurations; he and players often tune it out during play because they are concentrating on the game.

"It's like you have tunnel vision," Brown said. "The only things I really hear are the sneakers squeaking on the floor. You hear the players plain as day when they say something to you, and they hear you."

It's true that the Grizzlies used to have a slight disadvantage at home compared to the Spurs when it comes to noise level.

"Because of the shape of The Pyramid, all the noise goes up to the cone," Grizzlies owner Michael Heisley said after game two. "We won't have that problem next year ['04-'05] when we move into our new building [FedExForum]. You'll notice the difference with the improved acoustics and a different speaker system."

IT LOOKED LIKE IT WAS GOING IN

On the night that Griz owner Michael Heisley sang the national anthem as promised, and then-Griz coach Hubie Brown received his

Making the playoffs for the first time in '03-'04 had Griz fans rockin' The Pyramid.
© 2004 NBA Entertainment. Photo by Joe Murphy

NBA "Coach of the Year" award for 2003-04, Mike Miller could have written the perfect ending.

Instead, he stood frozen in a spot, 24 feet dead in front of the Grizzlies basket. He stared. He wondered. He wished—all while a disappointed sellout crowd of 19,351 filed out of The Pyramid after exhaling.

Miller's three-pointer, which could have stolen a victory, bounced cruelly off the left-back side of the rim, dooming the Griz to a 95-93 loss to the Spurs that put Memphis at a 3-0 deficit.

"I thought it was in, to be honest with you," Miller said. "I knew they didn't want to foul in that situation. I just tried to get as far as I could down court, and it hit the backside of the rim."

AND ALMOST A YEAR LATER, THIS ONE DID

Mike Miller didn't think his shooting stroke was that slow.

After much discussion, Miller's long-range jumper at the buzzer counted as the game-winner as the Griz edged the Spurs, 94-92, just before the end of the '04-'05 regular season.

The Grizzlies had the ball on their end of the court with 1.4 seconds left, plenty of time for Miller to get an inbounds pass from Jason Williams, turn, and hit a 22-footer from the right wing.

But official David Jones started the clock eight-tenths of a second early when Williams faked a pass, instead of starting it when the ball touched Miller's hands. That's why the shot still appeared to be in Miller's hands as the game-ending red light flashed on the backboard and the buzzer sounded.

"Jason made a great pass," Miller said. "I didn't have time to do anything but catch and shoot. I told one of our guys that, if I didn't get that shot off in time, I must have the slowest trigger in the league."

BEHAVE YOURSELF

Griz owner Michael Heisley doesn't like to stay quiet during a game. Which is why in game two of his team's '05 playoff series at Phoenix, Heisley found himself uncomfortably muzzled in a second-row courtside seat, a tough assignment since Memphis lost 108-103, thanks to a huge free-throw discrepancy favoring the home team.

"Believe me, I didn't want to be that quiet," Heisley said. "The Suns let me use one of their owners' seats and one of the owners' mothers was sitting next to me. I didn't want to be that well-behaved."

SNAP, CRACKLE, POP

Late in a game against Houston a couple of seasons ago, the Rockets were being trounced by the Grizzlies and looking for an exit, guard Steve Francis, who suddenly decided to show some false hustle and chase a loose ball near press row.

Although he didn't quite get to the ball to save it, to stop his momentum, he propped a hand on the top edge of a laptop screen belonging to Ron Tillery, Grizzlies' beat writer for *The Commercial Appeal.*

Tillery had just about finished a game story that had to be filed as soon as the game ended, when Francis came flying to the edge of the press table, shattering his computer screen.

While a blank-faced Tillery assessed the damage, a smiling and smug Francis said, "Just bill the Rockets."

THE TRIPLE-DOUBLE

Before the '05-'06 season, there had been only three triple-doubles in the Grizzlies' history. All had taken place when the franchise was still in Vancouver, but it seemed that, if any Griz player would be the first to do it in Memphis, it would be Pau Gasol, especially in '05-'06, after Coach Mike Fratello decided the offense needed to be run through Gasol.

Gasol flirted with a triple-double several times, but he got beaten to the punch by the most unexpected of sources, teammate Mike Miller, and it happened in a game Miller didn't even start. Miller came off the bench against Sacramento in a 99-85 victory in January '06, and had 21 points, 10 rebounds, and 10 assists in 41 minutes.

"Those last two rebounds were the hardest rebounds to get," Miller said exhaling.

Miller got his 10th assist with 4:55 left on a feed to Hakim Warrick, and needed just two rebounds for the triple-double. He got his ninth rebound with 2:31 left and No. 10 with 1:24 left.

The three previous triple-doubles were by Blue Edwards in 1996 versus Dallas (15 points, 12 rebounds, 11 assists), Shareef Abdur-Rahim in 1997 at Phoenix (26 points, 10 rebounds, 10 assists), and Mike Bibby in 2000 versus Dallas (14 points, 11 rebounds, 11 assists).

"I was fortunate that a lot of guys finished shots," Miller said.

Teammate Shane Battier said he and his teammates were urging Miller on in the final minutes. "The chance to get a triple-double just snuck up on Mike," Battier said. "But when he got within two rebounds, we told him, 'Go to the boards, this is your chance.' When he got that 10th rebound, it was pretty cool."

Starting guard Eddie Jones wondered, "I don't know if anybody ever has come off the bench to get a triple-double."

NO SMOKING, PLEASE

What was supposed to be a sleepy Sunday afternoon home game against docile Charlotte at the FedExForum late in the '05-'06 season turned into a real barnburner. About five minutes before tip-off, a small fire flared in a food preparation cart in a freight elevator on the terrace level. The crowd awaiting the tip-off was evacuated from the building safely, with no injuries suffered, and the teams went to the loading docks—all except for Shane Battier. The Griz forward, still in his game uniform, went outside with the rest of the fans so he could enjoy the sunny day.

"The last time I heard, to evacuate means leave the building," Battier told Ron Tillery of *The Commercial Appeal* while sitting on the steps in front of the FedExForum.

After 90 minutes, the game resumed; and the Grizzlies defeated the visiting Bobcats, 102-95.

"That fire drill seemed to last for four hours, and then we were searching for energy," said Griz guard Mike Miller, who scored 20 points (14 in the second half) off the bench. "We made some shots, and our building got into it. It would have been easy for the crowd not to come back after the fire drill. They really helped us win this game."

DIRK THE JERK

In the face of an unfriendly FedExForum crowd, Dallas all-star forward Dirk Nowitzki scored 35 points helping his team a 90-83 win in early December '05.

What got the Griz fans in a tizzy over Nowizzy?

There was a lot of pregame yapping over Nowitzki's postgame comments on November 26 after Grizzlies' 112-92 victory in Dallas. After Pau Gasol's night of 36 points and 15 rebounds, Nowitzki said: "[Gasol] is a good player, but he's not that good. We should have had an answer for him."

Gasol didn't have much to say about Nowitzki's diss, but Griz guard Bobby Jackson had Gasol's back.

"I don't even know why [Nowitzki's] talking," Jackson said. "He's probably the softest guy in the industry. I don't like guys who talk, and, you know, they're not a hardcore player. Don't talk about another player if you don't have that aggressiveness and aren't willing to mix it up. Dirk doesn't have that. So for him to say it, that goes right over my head. I don't respect anything he says. If it was [Kevin] Garnett or Tim Duncan, then okay. Dirk is one of the premier power forwards in the league. But he doesn't have that aggressiveness, and everybody knows it. Pau is getting there."

Nowitzki was booed every time he touched the ball. One Griz fan held a sign that read, "Dirk is a Jerk."

PLAYIN' CHICKEN

The game against the Warriors was well in hand in April '06, but FedExForum fans wanted the Grizzlies to hit 100 so they could cash in a game-program promotion for two free pieces of chicken.

Griz guard Bobby Jackson grabbed the drumstick from the bucket, so to speak, when he launched and hit a three-pointer with 37 seconds left for the final points in a 100-75 win. Griz coach Mike Fratello wasn't thrilled about Jackson taking what he felt was a needless shot.

"I wasn't jumping up and down calling for the three," Fratello said. "What are we trying to accomplish [shooting that shot]?"

"The way I was shooting lately, I didn't know if I should shoot it," said Jackson. "I was glad for everyone to get two pieces of chicken and a biscuit."

EDGING AHEAD OF HUBIE

When the Griz beat Milwaukee 100-90 in April '06, Griz coach Mike Fratello passed Hubie Brown as the franchise's all-time winningest coach. The fact Fratello did it in less than two seasons indicates how bad the franchise was before it moved from Vancouver to Memphis before the start of the 2001-02 season.

"I feel flattered I was around long enough to have the opportunity to coach these guys," Fratello said. "There were some very fine coaches before me, but I feel sorry for an expansion franchise, because it has to keep moving pieces around. Before I got here, the pieces were set. So it makes it a bit easier."

THE BIGGEST HEARTBREAK

There had been close playoff losses before, such as the aforementioned game three in the first-round series against the Spurs in '04, when Mike Miller's three-pointer at the buzzer missed, sealing a 95-93 Griz loss in The Pyramid. And there was the game two loss at Phoenix in '05, when the Grizzlies led by five points with 4:18 left, then the Suns scored nine straight points in a 108-103 victory. Miller missed a deep three with 6.3 seconds left that could have tied the game at 106-106.

But on the hurt scale, those losses were nothing compared to game three of the '06 first-round series against the Mavericks in FedExForum.

Until the last two minutes, the Grizzlies had done what they needed to do to win their first playoff game ever. They controlled tempo, they shot well, and they answered every Mavs' push. The Grizzlies led 76-72 with 37.6 seconds left in regulation. Yet, after Jason Terry made one free throw, he missed the second, and Mavs' backup center Erick Dampier tipped the ball to a teammate; so Dallas called timeout.

On the ensuing possession, a missed Dallas drive resulted in a scramble for the ball. Dampier batted it outside to Dirk Nowitzki, who nailed the three from the top of the key for a 76-76 tie.

Memphis rushed downcourt. Point guard Chucky Atkins got to the basket and missed a drive at the buzzer as the game went into overtime. The Grizzlies and the crowd of 17,871 seemed deflated. Dallas came out in the extra period, took the lead with Nowitzki quickly scoring five of his game-high 36 points, and the Mavs won 94-89.

"That's just the way sports works," former Griz forward Shane Battier lamented. "The ball bounces in a weird way to the best guy on their team. You almost knew he was going to make that shot. Call it karma, call it whatever."

"Damp knocked it out to me, and I really hadn't shot three-ball well all night," explained Nowitzki. "I took a dribble to my left, got rid of [Pau] Gasol, and I thought about tying the game. The shot didn't feel that great when it left my hand."

6

PASSING THROUGH

THANKS (SOME OF YOU) FOR STOPPING IN...

F ree agency has made all professional sports transient, and the Grizzlies have had their share of players make rest stops with the franchise. Some players, like Jason Williams, won't be forgotten. Others, such as the oft-injured Michael Dickerson and Bryant "Big Country" Reeves will be remembered for what might have been.

Here some of the faces that called Memphis home:

MICHAEL DICKERSON

(Acquired by the Grizzlies in August 1999 in a three-team trade with Houston and Orlando; retired October 2003.)

Just after the Grizzlies handed Dickerson a six-year, $43-million deal on October 30, 2001, he sustained what was thought to be a strained right-groin injury weeks later, which was diagnosed as a stress fracture near his right groin.

When he was healthy, former Griz guard Michael Dickerson scored bunches of points in a hurry. © 2001 NBA Entertainment. Photo by Fernando Medina

The likeable Dickerson, who missed almost all of the 2001-02 season, worked unbelievably hard to return the next season, then sustained what was termed a sports hernia. He played in just six games in 2002-03 before announcing his retirement on October 25, 2003, taking with him the remaining five years' worth of money on his contract.

"Things just didn't work out, and God has a plan for everyone," said Dickerson, who averaged 16.7 points in 162 games with the Griz as a shooting guard.

TONY MASSENBURG

(Acquired by the Grizzlies in a trade from Boston in October 1997; traded to Houston in '99; signed as a free agent with the Grizzlies in August 2000; waived by the Grizzlies in October 2002.)

Massenburg was the consummate professional and the only player in the history of the Grizzlies to leave and re-sign with the team as a free agent. Unfortunately for him, as the talent level improved in Memphis, he became expendable.

"I didn't know things would change so quickly," Massenburg said. "I knew there would be some changes. We had some guys who played together for a few years, but I knew the organization wanted to change the mind-set of the players."

Three years after Massenburg was waived by the Grizzlies, he landed with the Spurs, where he won an NBA championship ring in '04-'05.

BO OUTLAW

(Acquired by the Grizzlies in a trade from the Suns in September 2003; waived by the Grizzlies in October '04)

There was nothing aesthetically pretty about former Grizzlies forward Bo Outlaw as a basketball player.

"Do you see anything pretty about my game except my brand-new shoes?" the affable Outlaw said with a laugh.

But when your team was wheezing on the offensive end and defending its basket like Custer's Last Stand, Outlaw's scrappy style could be very beautiful. The messier the game, the better Outlaw played—and it drove

Tony Massenburg is the only Grizzly in history to leave the team and later in his career re-sign with the Griz as a free agent. © 2002 NBA Entertainment. Photo by Fernando Media

The beauty of former Griz forward Bo Outlaw was his hustle.
© 2003 NBA Entertainment. Photo by Joe Murphy

opponents crazy. How could they be shown up by a guy who had one of the ugliest shots in the NBA?

Outlaw's tireless hustle kept him in the league for 13 seasons (through the '05-'06 season) with four different teams after going undrafted out of the University of Houston in 1993. At 6-foot-8, 220 pounds, he was an undersized power forward who couldn't play the perimeter because he had virtually no shooting range. But he banged, bumped, and grinded. Former Dallas guard Michael Finley, who called Outlaw's shooting form "the worst in the NBA," added, "Maybe if he had a good shot, he wouldn't be able to do all those other things."

Scoring was not Outlaw's thing, and it wasn't why the Griz got him in a trade from the Suns on September 30, 2003, along with Jake Tsakalidis.

"Everywhere I've played, people know it wasn't because I'm going to give you 20 a night," said Outlaw. "I just go play, and I play hard. I hope people see it. Some people do and some people don't. My teammates appreciate me, though, and that's all that counts."

"He's very deceptive and a unique player in a very unconventional way," Shane Battier said. "His jump shot isn't the prettiest, but he knows how to spin shots off the backboard. He knows how to play the game the best way for him."

Outlaw, the only Grizzly player older than 30 on the '03-'04 playoff team, said he certainly hopes his years in the league have given him wisdom. And as for those crazy spinning hooks with either hand?

"I can't explain it," Outlaw said. "I'm not the biggest guy down there [in the post], so I've got to have a few tricks to find ways to make shots."

Outlaw wasn't too bitter about being waived by the Grizzlies in preseason '04, since they paid him approximately $6.6 million, honoring the remaining year on his contract. Plus, he was picked up by one of his old teams, the Suns, who were one of the best teams in the NBA in '04-'05.

JAMES POSEY

(Signed as a free agent in July '03; traded to Miami in August '05)

Posey spent just two years with the Grizzlies from 2003 to 2005, but he was the heart and soul of the first playoff team in '04. With his long arms, high motor, and fearlessness, he could turn games on a dime with

Former Griz swingman James Posey was the heart and soul of the '03-'04 playoff team. © 2003 NBA Entertainment. Photo by Rocky Widner

his defense, his slashes to the hoop, and an underrated three-point shot. His work ethic was unmatched as well—he was usually the last player to leave the practice court.

The 6-foot-8 swingman, who starred at Xavier in college, said he always wanted to become a crime-scene investigator after his pro career. He had taken several forensic science courses in college, and found it fascinating. He said he applied that knowledge to the way he approached playing defense.

"Defense is a lot like forensic science," Posey said. "It's a lot of detail, trying to see things beforehand, putting it together, then going out and doing it. That's all I try to do—think and be a step ahead."

After a fabulous first year with the Griz in which he was second on the team in scoring and a candidate for the NBA's Most Improved Player Award, he spent the majority of his second season hurt with various injuries, starting with a sprained foot in the preseason. He was traded to Miami along with Jason Williams before the '05-'06 season in the deal to get Eddie Jones, and played a key role off the bench in Miami's 2006 NBA title.

BRYANT "BIG COUNTRY" REEVES

(The first player ever drafted in Grizzlies franchise history as the sixth overall pick in the '95 NBA draft; retired January '02.)

Bryant Reeves was supposed to be the cornerstone of the franchise, a 7-foot, 275-pound center who could, at the very least, throw his weight around. His salary was astronomical—$11.5 million in '01-'02, $13 million in '02-'03 and $14.4 million in '03-'04—for someone who didn't come to close to averaging double figures in points and rebounds. The six-year deal worth $64.5 million Reeves signed in the summer of '97 simply killed the growth of the franchise.

Reeves came to Memphis with a hurt back and became the world's largest invisible man. Three degenerative discs in his back began touching in his spinal column, causing tingling in his feet. He seemed to stay in treatment for several months. The pain was so bad, he said, that some days he couldn't get out of bed. Because he was never well enough to play a regular-season game in Memphis before deciding after the 2001-02

Bryant Reeves stayed in Memphis just long enough to play an '01-'02 exhibition game, then collect paychecks after a career-ending back injury.
© 2001 NBA Entertainment. Photo by Glenn James

season to retire, the Grizzlies were able to file an insurance claim covering 80 percent of Reeves' income.

Even when he was healthy, Reeves had plenty of critics.

"My experience is, to be good at basketball, you've got to like to play basketball. You have to want to be good. I have yet to see that from Big Country," basketball Hall of Famer and television analyst Bill Walton once said of Reeves.

STROMILE SWIFT

(Drafted No. 2 overall in the 2000 draft; signed with Houston as a free agent in August 2005; traded back to the Grizzlies prior to the 2006 season.)

If there was anyone who appreciated the Grizzlies' first run to the playoffs in '03-'04, it was Stromile Swift, who was the last man standing from the Grizzlies' days in Vancouver. When the Grizzlies opened their first season in Memphis in 2001-02, the 6-foot-9 Swift was one of six holdovers who made the move from north of the border.

However, one by one, all were traded or waived.

Swift, the second-overall pick in the 2000 draft, carried the banner into the Grizzlies' first ever playoff appearance for all those players who suffered through lousy season after lousy season during the franchise's first six years of existence in Vancouver.

"I've seen the worst," Swift said. "So to come from Vancouver—from that losing situation to a winning team that has made the playoffs—I'm happy."

While it's true Swift only spent his rookie season in Vancouver, it was enough for him to get a taste of a heavy dose of losing that he had never experienced previously. He had been on winning teams in high school in Shreveport, Louisiana; and at LSU, where he led the Tigers to the regional semifinals of the NCAA tournament in 2000 during his sophomore season. That's when he decided to go pro and ended up in the NBA with a franchise that had never sniffed a winning season.

"I was always used to winning in high school and in college, so it was kind of frustrating being in that situation," Swift said. "But I was happy to learn from guys on our team like Shareef [Abdur-Rahim], Grant Long, Tony Massenburg, and Ike Austin. They really helped me stay focused with the stuff I had to deal with. The toughest part of being a rookie is the mental part. For 82 games, you go against the best in the world. And you have to deal with off-the-court situations. I had my family [from Louisiana] visit me a few times my rookie year."

Swift averaged 4.9 points and 3.6 rebounds, and 16.4 minutes for a Grizzlies team that finished 23-59. He never had a chance to play extensively, though in a couple of back-to-back games late in the season, he did lead the team in rebounding. Most of the time, he looked very much like a rookie, uncertain where to go on certain plays. Other times he displayed his phenomenal athletic ability that brought Vancouver fans out of their seats with his dunks.

"I thought the fans in Vancouver were great," Swift said. "Now, there were a lot of people who didn't come to the games and didn't buy tickets, but the fans that came to the games were good fans. They supported us like Memphis fans support us—though Memphis is more of a basketball town."

That made it tough on Swift and the rest of the Grizzlies in their final two months in Vancouver. As word began to leak out that majority owner Michael Heisley was looking to move the team to a more basketball-friendly city, the Grizzlies' season went south.

They lost 16 of their last 19 games, including losing streaks of nine and six games. Their last home game in Vancouver was typical of their season—a 100-95 loss to Houston in which Grizzlies seemed on the verge of victory but failed to make any plays in the stretch. In fact, the 2000-2001 Grizzlies were 3-17 in games decided by five points or fewer.

"We were in a lot of close games, we just couldn't pull it off," Swift said. "We had good players, but the chemistry wasn't good on that team."

Swift had some breathtaking moments in Memphis. There was a stretch of games in the '02-'03 season where he had six straight double-doubles, picking up the slack for usual starting center Lorenzen Wright, who missed several games due to the death of his infant daughter.

But Swift finally became expendable because he simply didn't deliver a heartfelt effort night in and night out. There were more six-point, three-rebound games for Swift than 18-point, nine-rebound performances.

Finally, the Griz gave up on him, and he signed with the Rockets in the summer of '05. Houston was hoping Swift could be a starter to help center Yao Ming on the boards. Yet he proved to be as maddeningly inconsistent with the Rockets as he was with the Grizzlies, which is why they shipped him back to Memphis in their trade for Shane Battier on draft night '06.

EARL WATSON

(Signed by the Grizzlies as free agent in July 2002; signed as a free agent with Denver before the '05-'06 season.)

Watson was a more than able backup for point guard Jason Williams. Blessed with astounding athleticism—he once pinned a shot on the backboard attempted by 7-foot-6 Dallas center Shawn Bradley—he often was a fourth-quarter savior with his lockdown defense.

Two great traits that remained consistent with Watson were his fearlessness and his professionalism. By playing collegiately at UCLA, Watson learned not to back down from anybody, including teammate and good friend Baron Davis, who has enjoyed an outstanding NBA career with several teams.

"My four years playing at UCLA, I worked out with Magic Johnson every summer," Watson said. "He taught me how to run the point. I don't know if you can find a bigger name than Magic to go against."

Then starting his pro career in Seattle and practically being adopted by future Hall of Fame point guard Gary Payton, Watson advanced his basketball knowledge.

"You can't be selfish in this game," Watson said. "You can't think the game owes you. When that happens, things go wrong for you. You get snake-bit."

BONZI WELLS

(Traded to the Grizzlies from Portland in December 2003; traded to Sacramento in August '05.)

The day that Wells met the Memphis media for the first time, December 4, 2003, after being traded from Portland, where he did everything from making an obscene gesture at a fan to spitting on an opposing player, he vowed, "I'm really a good guy."

Earl Watson had the quickness and hops to beat anybody off the dribble, including the Sixers' Allen Iverson. © 2005 NBA Entertainment. Photo by Jesse D. Garrabrant

Well, he was as long as he was guaranteed minutes in Hubie Brown's 10-man rotation.

"Bonzi Wells is not a mystery," Brown said at the time. "He's been a starter for six years. With us, Bonzi has accepted his role and played very well."

Wells' stay in Memphis came to an ugly end. As the '04-'05 season drew to a close, Griz coach Mike Fratello gave Wells infrequent and erratic playing time. During one game after being pulled, Wells yanked off his sweatbands and headbands, and angrily tossed them into the FedExForum crowd.

While Wells kept saying the right things in front of the cameras and reporters, his locker-room sniping did him in. The day of game four, the final playoff game against the Suns, Wells was told by the Grizzlies not to bother coming to the last game of the season.

"Bonzi and I decided that it was in the best interest of the team, that it was in the best interest of both parties," Fratello said at the time.

In early August '05, the Grizzlies traded Wells to Sacramento in a deal that landed guard Bobby Jackson in Memphis.

JASON WILLIAMS

(Traded to the Grizzlies from Sacramento in June 2001; traded to Miami in August '05.)

Like Wells, things were grand for Williams under Hubie Brown. The ol' coach and the young gunslinger who matured as a ball-handler but regressed in his shot selection formed a partnership of trust.

But when Brown left early in the '04-'05 season and new coach Mike Fratello ditched Brown's 10-man rotation—guaranteeing those men at least 24 minutes of playing time per game—Williams found himself angry that he was being benched late in games. Fratello, the fourth coach in Williams' NBA life, perhaps had the best description of dealing with the temperamental point guard.

"He has leadership qualities, but only when he wants to apply them," Fratello said. "If he did some of the stuff I've seen him do some nights, and did it for 82 games, he'd be great."

The beginning of the end for Williams came after a late-season win over Charlotte in April 2005. The Grizzlies were trying to cling to a

Former Griz point guard Jason Williams never held anything back on or off the court. © 2005 NBA Entertainment. Photo by Joe Murphy

playoff spot, and Williams was upset about being benched the last 17 minutes of the game

So afterwards, in the locker room, he unleashed a string of profanities at Fratello, who fined Williams and didn't start him the next game. Fratello filed the incident, even though Williams played well in the playoffs, when the Griz were swept 4-0 by the Suns.

"When Mike and I got into it at that one game back at home, I think he understood that was just me venting," Williams said when the playoffs concluded. "I want to be on the floor the whole game. I think everybody wants to, and if they didn't, there might be something wrong with them. But it hasn't been much different. He lets me play, and I think Hubie let me play, too. But in the fourth quarter, if I'm not in there, I get frustrated.

"I think Mike let it go. I don't know that he's let it go. It seems not to bother us. Our relationship is okay as long as I go out and play hard. I think we have a working relationship. It comes from respect. The guy has been around so long, and he knows so much about the game," Williams continued. "When we went at it, it was a mistake by me. But there's nothing I can do about it now. I did it—that's the way I do things. I'm not saying I'm right. Hey, I'm human. I just want to play and win. I understood sometimes why he takes me out. He should. As I said, I want to play the whole game, and I'm sure everybody else out here wants to play the whole game, too. Everybody thinks we have a tough job. Mike's got a helluva tough job. He's got to keep 15 people happy. I'm just trying to keep me happy."

Williams wasn't happy with anybody. Following what became his last game as a Grizzly, a game four-playoff loss to the Suns in Memphis, a wild-eyed Williams confronted *Memphis Commercial Appeal* sports columnist Geoff Calkins in the locker room.

After calling Calkins an unspeakable name, he grabbed Calkins' pen and said, "You ain't getting no quotes tonight, homeboy."

"I write what I want," Calkins said.

Teammate Mike Miller stepped in, pulled Williams away as he continued to shout, "Where do you live?"

The Grizzlies simply didn't want to put up with Williams anymore, so they traded him to Miami along with James Posey in August 2005 in the Eddie Jones deal.

Even with the Heat, Williams was spouting off about his time with the Grizzlies. When he returned to play the Grizzlies, as fate would have it, in the '05-'06 season opener, he was asked how it felt to be back in Memphis. He replied, "I miss South Beach."

Yet, Williams had the last laugh in the end. The player who had bitched his way out of every bad playing situation finally griped his way on to a team that won the NBA championship. When the Heat won the '06 league title over the Mavs, the irony was that Williams had now won the same amount of rings as a player—one—as Jerry West.

7

THE LOGO

WEST MOVES EAST

Michael Heisley didn't get to be a multimillionaire by accident. He does his homework, knows how to read people, and doesn't mind being a sly dog every now and then. More importantly, the Chicago CEO of The Heico Companies L.L.C. knows how to close the deal.

So when Heisley went to Los Angeles to visit Jerry West in the spring of 2002, his purpose was to seek advice on several matters from West, the former Lakers star and retired team vice-president of basketball operations. West had advised Heisley before when Heisley bought the Grizzlies in April 2000. Yet, before this trip to the West Coast, Heisley had read that West was interested in getting back in the NBA.

For most of the day in West's home, the men talked. Finally, Heisley asked West if it was true that he was considering returning to the game. When West admitted as much, Heisley, being the good salesman, knew exactly how to sell his situation to the ultra-competitive West.

"I told him that if he came to Memphis, he'd be coming to a franchise that had no success in history," Heisley said. "So if he got us to the playoffs, it would be one of the crowning achievements of his career."

And that's exactly how it played out.

"I've had more gratification, personally, watching what's happening here than maybe even when we won championships in Los Angeles," said West, who was part of nine NBA titles as a player and in the Lakers front office in 42 years with the organization. "That's because, in Los Angeles, you almost always have perfect teams. Here in Memphis, we don't have a perfect team, and the job is complex with fewer dollars to work with."

When word began to leak that West might be considering a move to Memphis after two years as a consultant with the Lakers—a semi-retirement he had chosen after self-admitted job burnout—it was one of the most emotional decisions of West's life.

"It was difficult to break an umbilical cord with a team that I had been involved with since 1960," West said. "I'm a real loyal person; people that I like and care about, I'll do anything for them. I didn't think I'd ever work again, but the competitive part of me was a lot stronger than I thought. As a consultant for the Lakers, I wasn't called very much, and I felt as if I was taking somebody's money for nothing. I'm not built that way.

"I'd gotten bored living the good life with no stress or pressure," West added. "When I started studying this thing in Memphis, it was the ultimate challenge for me. Could I make a difference? I can't tell you how many people I knew in basketball told me, 'What the hell you are doing? … Of all places to go.' I said, 'That's what I want to do.'"

THE DNA OF A WINNER

You'd think that a guy who was raised as a country boy in West Virginia, like West, would grow up to be a conservative, laidback guy, someone who didn't take risks—someone who rarely thought outside of the box.

On his way to the Naismith Basketball Hall of Fame as one of the greatest players in NBA history and one of its highest-scoring guards, West discovered several things about himself:

There hasn't been a tougher challenge in Griz President Jerry West's career than improving what had been the worst team in the NBA.
© 2004 NBA Entertainment. Photo by Joe Murphy

—He liked the responsibility of being in charge: "As a player, you had some control, and if you're good enough, you had a lot of control. In a front-office position, you can go out and make the best possible decision you think you can make, and move forward. Someone has to make the decision."

—He relished a challenge: "I don't think men are worth a damn unless you have a challenge in your life. I think the thing that has always driven me is people telling me, 'No.' When I was little, people told me I couldn't do this and couldn't do that. I've always looked at it differently, I take 'no' as meaning 'yes.'

"I've always been a goal-setter. When you set goals, you get knocked down a lot. Goals allow you to get out of bed, compete, and excel. If you don't have any goals, you're not going to get out of bed. I set lofty goals. It makes you extend yourself, it makes you reach a bit higher, and it stretches you. Everything that you want to accomplish, you won't accomplish it without goals. After the Lakers, I didn't think I'd ever work again. But it finally all got to me—the competitive part of me was a lot stronger than I thought it was."

—He didn't like to play it safe: "I think it's so easy to protect yourself in this league. I'm not that way. I'm not afraid to make mistakes because I've made them. I remember the day I was hired here in Memphis, I was asked, 'What kind of plan do you have—a one-year plan, a two-year plan, or four- or five-year plan?' I don't believe in those things. I think that's a wrong message to send to your fans, an easy way to protect your ass. I'm not into protecting myself."

THE KNACK

How does West have the knack, more often than not, of ultimately making the right personnel move?

West really can't tell you, other than he listens to many people around him, but then often makes a decision he knows that is "… questioned even by a lot of people you work with."

Owner Michael Heisley said that, as a fan, even he has disagreed with some of West's decisions.

"For instance, when he hired Hubie [Brown as coach early in 2002-03], I thought he'd lost his mind," Heisley said. "But every reason he gave me for hiring Hubie—he's a great teacher, disciplinarian, and motivator—was exactly right. It's why Jerry has 100-percent authority over making all the decisions in the basketball operations. He might call me from time to time to discuss something, but I always tell him to do what he wants to do."

Gary Colson, West's longtime friend and his assistant with the Grizzlies, has seen the West magic play out repeatedly.

"Jerry shocks me when he picks people," Colson said. "He'll come up with a name. He'll say, 'Gary, I really like him.' I'd say, 'Who did ya say?' Then I go look it up and say, 'Dadgum, well … James Posey.' Jerry sees things nobody else sees."

Mitch Kupchak, now the Lakers GM who learned under West, said one of the main things West taught him was to go with your gut on tough decisions.

"There are a lot of opinions out there from a lot of people," Kupchak said. "You have to be careful not to be swayed. Jerry taught me not to be afraid to follow my instincts."

Possessing such instinctive brilliance can have drawbacks, especially when you start winning. It can be assumed the more West lives up to his reputation as one of the best wheelers-and-dealers in the business, the harder it is for him to find willing parties to get deals done.

"You've got general managers thinking that 'Why would I want a player that Jerry West doesn't want?'" said Bill Walton, ESPN color analyst and a Hall of Famer. "That proved to be true with the deal he made with Orlando. Orlando gives up Mike Miller for Drew Gooden, who [wasn't] very good in Orlando, and Gordan Giricek, who has already moved on to Utah."

West sometimes becomes mentally drained chasing talent.

"These jobs become more difficult mentally when you need a certain player," West said. "You look around and wonder, 'How in the hell are we going to get that piece? We have to get another rebounder; we're the worst defensive rebounding team in the league.' Getting that piece is what frustrates you, but that's what drives you."

I WANNA TAKE YOU HIGHER

The hiring of West raised eyebrows across the NBA. It also raised the bar in the Memphis business community.

"I'm involved in many areas of the community, and the Grizzlies getting Jerry West set the expectations for success higher," said Gayle Rose, part of the pursuit team in Memphis that got the Grizzlies to move from Vancouver. "There are a lot of people in this city now in business and other areas saying, 'We need a Jerry West-type.' There's an expectation now that it's no longer ok to limit the possibilities, that in this city we can expect for and ask for the best, and that they really might consider moving here. It's raised the possibility that maybe we weren't so bad after all."

No doubt, West misses some things about Los Angeles. He misses the anonymity of being a big fish in an ocean, a place where people call him "Jerry" and not "Mr. West." He traded golf dates and cards nights with friends for time spent at the office building a franchise. West moved from a place where "… there's 10 million people you can sell season tickets to, where the successful history of the Lakers made the playing field even more uneven," he said.

The challenge for West, something he never faced before in Los Angeles, is that he's building more than a team. He's building a product, and the two have to go hand-in-hand.

"Coming here, you have to be more conscious of the dollars spent," he said. "Regardless of what market you are in, the owner has a right to make a profit. And the thing that troubles me is that hasn't happened."

But West certainly doesn't believe it's impossible. He has seen small-market franchises such as Utah and Indiana go deep into the playoffs—even make the Finals. That's why he's not ready for anyone to pat him or the franchise on the back for a job well done.

"I just don't want to have a playoff team," he said. "I want to build a team that endures the test of time and not just be a one-year wonder. We want to create excitement. We want to build a franchise this city will embrace, that people will clamor to watch play."

LIFE IN MEMPHIS

West has tried to make himself as invisible as possible, and he has enjoyed the laidback style of living in the South.

"The people are wonderful here in Memphis," West said. "I grew up in the South [West Virginia], and this is what I'm used to—people who are friendly and gregarious. Memphis is a big town, but a small town. One of the things I do miss about Los Angeles is I was Jerry in Los Angeles. Here, I'm Mr. West. I'd still prefer to be Jerry. That would be a Godsend for me."

Colson said it's hard for West to throttle back.

"Jerry eats like a 24-second shot clock is running," Colson said. "You better not talk while he's eating, because he'll be asking for the check before you're halfway through. And if you're going somewhere with him, don't ever drive. Even if you're in your own car, just give him the keys. Mitch Kupchak once told me that if Jerry's venting, it might last 30 minutes. It might last three days. The main thing is to listen and don't get in an argument. It's good for him."

Colson recalls one of the first days in Memphis when he and West decided to break from the office and grab some lunch.

"We take this little side street, and this guy sees us," Colson recalled with a laugh, "and he starts screaming, 'Jerry West, *I can't believe it! Halleluiah!*'"

PLAYOFF PAIN

Check the all-time statistics for the NBA Finals, and you'll find West's name is sprinkled throughout like Tabasco on red beans and rice.

- Fourth in scoring average at 30.5.
- First in points scored (1,679), field goals made (612) and attempted (1,333), free throws made (455) and attempted (551).
- Second in minutes (2,375) and games (55).

Yet, West will tell you the only statistic he remembers from all those games in the Finals.

"I'm not proud of fact I played in nine championship series and won only one of them [in 1972]," West said. "The most painful moments in my life occurred in some of my very best moments as a player. It's probably something that has left a lot of internal scars on me; it's the thing that has driven me all my life … to lose a couple of times when I know we had the best team, and we didn't win."

West said losing a playoff series as a player was a drain and a motivation.

"It made me harder, more determined, but also made me want to give up sometimes," West said. "Because you put so much into it, and regardless of what you do as an individual, you still don't win. Probably regardless of how I played, I can't tell you how many times at the height of my career I didn't want to play another basketball game. I didn't want to compete again—it hurt that much."

How much? West ranks the worst two moments of his career as losing in the NCAA championship game to California in '59 (71-70) and in the NBA Finals in '69 to Boston (4-3 after leading 2-0 and 3-2, losing Game

Seven in Los Angeles, 108-106). Both times, West was named the Most Valuable Player, but it just didn't matter.

"I have no idea where it is," West said of his Finals MVP trophy.

Even the year West finally won a championship, in '72 over the Knicks, he deemed his performance sub-par since he only averaged 22.9 points in the playoffs that year.

"It was the first time I'd played so terrible—for me—in the playoffs," West said. "I was delighted that for the city of Los Angeles that we won because of so many previous disappointments. Yet, after that season, I really wondered if I should play anymore. I'm the most self-critical person in the world. Some nights, I'd play almost a perfect game, and I'd still be critical. That's not a good way to live your life. I played out of fear, fear that we weren't going to win, fear that I wasn't going to contribute to my unusual standards. Consequently, I never really enjoyed any success I had."

TRACKING HURRICANE JERRY

Almost every move that West has made since he was hired by the Grizzlies has helped the franchise take another step forward. But it gets tougher and tougher. Most NBA teams know West's reputation for spotting something in a player they may not see. Even if a team wants to get rid of a player, and West wants that player, suddenly that team has cold feet.

As deals fall through, West starts over again. Here are some of the moves he has made to better a franchise that was once the welcome mat on which every NBA team wiped its feet:

—Hired 69-year-old Hubie Brown to replace Sidney Lowe, and a season later Brown won NBA Coach of the Year as the Griz went to the playoffs for the first time in franchise history.

"I didn't throw a dart, but I think circumstances dictate who you hire in this league," West said. "I knew the way Hubie teaches, the discipline he instills. His discipline is different. Everyone thinks he's a tough guy, but he's soft. He's mellowed, and our players know how good he is."

—In the 2002 draft, he picked Drew Gooden and Gordan Giricek, then traded them before mid-season for Mike Miller, a former league

Rookie of the Year, who has developed into one of the NBA's best outside shooters and the league's '05-'06 Sixth Man of the Year.

—In August 2003, West's only free agent acquisition was signing Houston forward James Posey, whose career statistics revealed he was little more than a spot-role defensive specialist. With the Grizzlies, he emerged as the team's Most Valuable Player of its '03-'04 playoff team, the heart and soul of the never-say-die-mayhem he created on both ends of the court.

—On September 30, 2003, West traded three nondescript contributors to Phoenix on the eve for center Jake Tsakalidis and forward Bo Outlaw. Tsakalidis has been slow to develop, but Outlaw delivered suffocating defense on the 2003-04 playoff team.

—On December 3, 2003, West sent struggling three-point shooter Wesley Person, a conditional first-round pick, and some cash to Portland for alleged bad-boy Bonzi Wells. Wells seemed genuinely humbled that West had enough faith in him to acquire him. Wells played hard and was a model citizen until Brown left early in the 2004-05 season. That's when new coach Mike Fratello abandoned Brown's 10-man rotation. With his playing time becoming erratic, Wells became a locker-room malcontent, and he was traded to Sacramento in August 2005.

—In a four-day period in August 2005, West got three 30-year-old-plus veterans who filled backcourt and leadership needs. He got Bobby Jackson in a trade from Sacramento for Wells; he got Eddie Jones in a trade from Miami for Jason Williams and James Posey; and he signed free-agent point guard Damon Stoudamire.

—After Stoudamire's '05-'06 season ended with a torn patella tendon, West was able to get seven-year veteran Chucky Atkins off waivers from the Wizards in late January. Atkins had started all 82 games in '04-'05 for the Lakers, and to pick up a point guard of his caliber for the rest of the season without having to make a trade was a slick move.

"I live my life by instincts," West said. "Sometimes you have to follow your instincts. Sometimes, it takes courage when you get criticized when you do things like that. It's not easy to do that. I know people around me think I'm crazy—and I *am* crazy. I just have a different insight from other people to what I think is important. Sometimes it works; sometimes it doesn't."

WEST FANS ARE EVERYWHERE

Suns coach Mike D'Antoni, a West Virginia native, grew up as a huge fan of Jerry West. D'Antoni was such a fan that, as a rookie guard in 1973-74 for the Kansas City-Omaha Kings playing against the Lakers, he couldn't help cheering for his hero.

"We were playing the Lakers. Jerry's made just one-of-12 shots, and he had sat out most of the game with an abdominal strain," D'Antoni said. "But at the end, since it was a one-point game, they put Jerry back in the game. Everybody knew he was going to get the ball. Everybody was screaming his name. He let the shot go, and before it even went in, he turned and laughed as he ran down court.

"I jumped off the bench and threw my arms in the air," D'Antoni remembered. "Then I looked around and realized where I was."

8

EVERYBODY LOVES HUBIE

BACK IN THE SADDLE AGAIN

The only thing more shocking than his hiring on November 12, 2002, was his abrupt departure on Thanksgiving Day two years later.

("One of the worst and most awkward days of my life," Griz president Jerry West would say.)

In between, though—in the 168 games that Hubie Brown coached the Grizzlies—each day was lesson for everyone around him. Ask him a question, and you got perspective and wisdom of man who had spent a lifetime breathing, living, and loving the game; and his players learned that playing for him wasn't overcomplicated.

"He tells you your job, and if you do your job there's no problems," said former Griz guard Bonzi Wells, who loved playing for Brown. "He demands respect. If there is some guy 200 feet away from him talking, and Hubie gives him that look, they'd better be quiet."

Hubie knew exactly who he was, stayed true to himself and never strayed.

"I'm a Type-A personality," Brown said. "Players can handle a Type-A personality, as long as you're fair and constructive. You can't yell at them without teaching them. You don't teach them as an individual. You teach them as a group. Like pro football, if one guy on a basketball team is out of sync, the group can't function."

THEY REALLY HIRED HUBIE?

When West practically pulled Brown out of a hat—he had spent 15 years away from coaching as an award-winning television analyst—several of the Grizzlies did a double-take when they heard the news that their new coach was 69 years old.

"No, it can't be him, he's a sports announcer," Griz center Lorenzen Wright recalled a telling a friend who called him with the news Brown had been hired. "Let me find out the name, who it really is."

Then-76ers coach Larry Brown didn't bat an eye when Brown was hired.

"I don't know who's in for a bigger shock, the players or Hubie," Larry Brown said. "I've seen him work at Michael's [Jordan] camp, and he gets after those older guys pretty enthusiastically."

WELCOME TO HUBIEBALL

Wright said it didn't take long to understand with Brown that it was Hubie's way or the highway.

"At our first practice, nobody knew how to take him," Wright recalled. "He was yelling, he was cursing. He was screaming, 'Get to this spot, get to that spot, get to this spot.' Nobody knew the reason those first few practices. Then, we started playing games. You get to those spots. You have open shots."

Griz swingman Shane Battier loved Brown's attention to detail.

"He always talked about spacing," Battier said. "On certain plays, he wanted us three feet from the free throw line—not four feet, not two feet. If we got it wrong, he'd stop practice and correct that one foot."

His team started to believe, even guard Jason Williams, whose lousy shot selection, wild passing, and penchant for playing soft defense got him benched in Sacramento, then traded.

Former Griz coach Hubie Brown demanded perfection from himself and everyone around him. © 2004 NBA Entertainment. Photo by Joe Murphy

He and Brown came to a quick, simple understanding.

"I don't care if a player has got a style, as long as he makes no turnovers," Brown said. "As soon as you turn the ball [over], then you've got to be accountable."

Williams responded with the lowest assists-to-turnover ratio of his career.

"Hubie doesn't accept anything but your best, and he gets the best out of me that way," Williams said of bonding with Brown. "He let me play my game. He's totally opposite of what I thought."

It was such an odd coupling that television analyst Bill Walton said, "It's like Aristotle teaching Eminem."

Brown's unparalleled basketball knowledge was a reason why the Grizzlies players—starved for victory, starved for a plan—bought into his philosophies almost immediately.

"There's nothing on the court he hasn't seen; he's got an answer for everything," Griz forward Pau Gasol said of Brown.

Brown also brought old-school toughness back from a day when players didn't tolerate much foolishness on the court.

"You got to tell a defender, 'The next time you hold me like that, you're going to get an elbow in the face,'" Brown said.

But as tough as Brown could be, he was still a softie at heart. Win or lose after a game, he'd shake the hands of his players.

"He was like a grandfather who'd whip your butt, but give you a "Good job, kid,'" Wright said.

NO, I'M NOT HUBIE BROWN, BUT I'D LIKE TO BE

In the first few days when Brown took over in Memphis, as the fans got used to his face and shock of white hair, Gary Colson, assistant to Jerry West, was a popular guy.

He and West were eating lunch at Huey's, a favorite downtown spot, where well-wishers were stopping by the table and complimenting Brown—actually Colson—for immediately improving the team. West sat back and played along just to gig Colson.

"We step outside of Huey's, this cab stops and the driver says to me, 'Coach Brown, good luck, thank you for coming to town,'" Colson said. "I thought, 'Being Hubie could work pretty well for me. But if he doesn't win, I'll have to dye my hair.'"

THE 10-MAN ROTATION

At the start of the 2003-04 season, there were many NBA skeptics were questioning Brown and his 10-man rotation. By February, when it became obvious the Grizzlies were the Cinderella story of the league, everyone wanted to know how Brown could use 10 players successfully every game.

And he told everyone—NBA stop after NBA stop after NBA stop. In what became almost a standard rant, it went like this: "These young guys write about this stuff, it's kind of amusing sometimes, but ... we don't tell anybody how to coach. There are guys with seven-man rotations. Now if you've been following your box scores this week, there are four teams in the league just rotating seven guys. Why? Because they're in a fight just holding their spots.

"Hey, whatever your philosophy is, that's great," Brown continued. "We just like to do this our way. We're not trying to convert anybody into this. I heard a guy say, 'This thing won't work in the playoffs.' ... Guys make all kinds of outlandish statements when they take a shot at what we're trying to do. But, see, we don't really care. The key thing from our first phone call is to develop the talent. ...

"Then, we get in the playoffs, the starters play more minutes, and the substitutes play less minutes. But this isn't new for us. You have to be fair. You have to be constructive. There has to be accountability with discipline. Then everybody can be on the same page. Fortunately, you can run this type of system, but you better have players. We have the style, the discipline and an expectation. We make them all accountable. I'm talking 15 guys, not 12. So if we have an injury we don't dwell on the injury. We have not had Mike Miller and Lorenzen Wright. A lot of teams would lose two starters of that quality and struggle. We're not worried about the guys stepping in and getting major minutes. We have guys who have played off the bench all year and getting minutes. So when a starter goes down, we have someone coming in and playing. …

"Pro sports, the fan wants his team to win. He can only handle so much. He can handle it if you have the injuries, but every game is close; and in the last three minutes, you have a chance to win. He can handle that, because now he knows the guys stepping up and playing are giving everything they have. We credit the players for all of this because our practices are very demanding and our games are very demanding. So no coach with any type of philosophy in pro sports wins without players. We're proud of where this group is right now, we're proud of every one of them. If they go down, the next guy taking their spot is a true player for us.

"What we try to do is fit them into our style," Brown continued. "We've been very fortunate since last November 12 when I took over this team, we have nine new guys out of 15. Every one of them was brought here by Jerry West. Jerry has great vision. And he sees the style. He never once brings a player here that can't play the style. As we all know, that's a key to the coaching staff. Now the coaching staff can continue a beat because all the guys play a style.

"When you get players who don't have the stamina, can't run the lanes, and do what we do from a defensive standpoint, well, if you made a mistake then you must move these people on. Well, that takes a lot of courage … in sports, in the business world etc., because the media and the fan base might like those players even though they don't fit. And you see it all the time in pro basketball. What happens is management sits on these players, they never get true chemistry, the team underachieves, and nobody is happy. He's not Mr. General Manager, he's not who he is, because he's worrying about what anyone else is thinking. He doesn't have the big picture always in perspective about making moves."

And then, finally, Hubie exhaled.

ONLY A STATE OF MIND

Brown wore his age proudly. He was part of a group of coaching throwbacks hired in various sports early this decade, such as 73-year-old

Florida Marlins manager Jack McKeon and 61-year-old Dallas Cowboys head coach Bill Parcells.

"The coaches that have been asked to come back and coach all had solid track records," Brown said in January 2004. "They all have philosophies; they all are extremely organized and disciplined. They all have a style. You've got to have a style. The most frightening thing in the corporate world and in athletics is to become 55 years old. All of a sudden, people are planning behind your back. You're not invited to meetings anymore. They buy you out, [then] you're out on the street, and you have to re-sell yourself. At 55, you should be at the height of your knowledge, at the top of your game. And all of a sudden people have doubts about you?"

Brown said that commanding respect, at any age, is the secret to success.

"It's like when you go back and think about who may have been the most influential teacher in your life," he said. "It could have been that little, old 95-pound English teacher who had complete command of the classroom from the moment she walked in. You were just in awe of her. Meanwhile, across the hall, there's a young 6-foot-5, 285-pound teacher, who has no control of his class. Guys are jumping out windows, and he doesn't command the respect to control them."

ARTIS KNOWS HUBIE

Artis Gilmore had to feel like he had stepped into a time machine. The former NBA center, as well as the center on Hubie Brown's 1975 ABA championship team with the Kentucky Colonels, visited Memphis to watch his old coach at work in Game 3 of the '04 playoffs.

"I don't think he's ever lost a beat," Gilmore said. "He's been able to transcend. He never left the game when he was a television analyst, and he breaks the game down to where the average person can understand it."

Gilmore played 18 years professionally—his first five in the ABA with Kentucky—before jumping to the NBA with Chicago in 1976-77. He averaged 17.1 points and 10.1 rebounds with four different NBA teams before retiring in 1988. As an ABA star, he averaged 22 points and 16 rebounds.

The year the Colonels won the league title, Gilmore averaged 24.2 points and 15.2 rebounds in the playoffs.

Gilmore said that Brown's strength as coach in the 1970s was the same as it was in 2004.

"He has tremendous communication skills and knowledge of the game," Gilmore said. "He's been pretty much the same. He calls the plays, keeps players under control, and gets the maximum out of each of his players. He gets his guys to buy in the system. When you do that, the end result is usually positive. Hubie has always had a positive impact on the game."

THEY THREW ME OUT?

In a February 2003 game against the Pacers, Brown had barely warmed his seat on the bench when he got thrown out of the game—and he wasn't even trying.

It played out this way. Brown wasn't happy that on his team's first three offensive possessions of the game, Pau Gasol (twice) and Lorenzen Wright once appeared to get fouled; but no calls were made by the officiating crew of Steve Javie, Sean Corbin, and Gary Zielinski. Finally, after Indiana's Jermaine O'Neal was called for the Pacers' first foul with 8:56 left after hacking Wright, Corbin approached the scorers table to announce the foul. Brown strayed slightly on the floor to talk to him.

Brown, in a calm voice, to Corbin: "All we want is a fake shake." Corbin looked at Brown with a blank stare and whistled him for a technical foul. Brown, who moved close to Corbin as the crowd began booing, said, "That's a technical? I didn't swear."

Javie, standing 40 feet away under the basket, said to Brown, "Hubie, that's enough. Sit down."

Brown didn't hear him. He repeated to Corbin, "Why is it a technical? I didn't swear."

Corbin to Brown: "You said it three times: 'It's a foul, make the call.'"

Javie, interrupting again: "I'm sick of this. I'm not listening to this. Bang! You're gone!"

Brown still didn't hear him. He had to be told by one of his assistants that he had been thrown out of the game. The Grizzlies, with assistant

Lionel Hollins taking Brown's place, beat the Pacers 108-103 in overtime. Afterward, Brown thanked Hollins for holding together the team, but was still puzzled why he was given an early boot.

"I could live with Corbin tossing me out of the game," Brown said. "But I was stunned when Javie, who's 40 feet away, throws me out, and he can't even hear the conversation I'm having [with Corbin]."

COACH OF THE YEAR

When Brown was named the NBA's Coach of the Year for the '03-'04 season, an honor he won back in 1978 when he coached the Atlanta Hawks, there wasn't a prouder group of guys than his team.

"If didn't win it, everybody would have said Hubie was cheated," Griz center Lorenzen Wright said.

Added swingman Shane Battier, "Coach Brown turned a franchise that knew futility and embarrassment into a playoff team."

FDR OR HUBIE?

Basketball Hall of Famer Bill Walton was a huge fan of the Grizzlies' turnaround under Brown and Jerry West.

"I saw a Hubie interview the other night on NBA-TV," Walton said during the '03-'04 season. "And I was like a little boy listening to one of Franklin Roosevelt's fireside chats on the radio."

DO IT HUBIE'S WAY

Brown often showed an abundance of patience with his young team. But if a player screwed up more than twice, he drew the line.

In a game early in 2002, rookie forward Drew Gooden had hit his first four shots but didn't run the offense on any of his shots.

"If you don't run the play," Brown said after angrily calling a timeout, "you're coming out."

In practice, he was a taskmaster. If a player blew an assignment and said, "My bad," old-school Hubie wasn't down with the street-ball apology.

"I hate the 'My bads,' so stop it," Hubie growled. "Just do your [bleeping] job."

Brown was unflappable when it came to coaching players who were problems for their previous teams, such as Jason Williams and Bonzi Wells. Of Wells, Brown said, "I've had guys that made him look like Mary Poppins. Okay? I've had some killers in my time who were all-league players."

THE STUNNING EXIT

Several things led to Brown's departure on Thanksgiving 2004. The stress of a poor start in his second full season didn't help, plus Jason Williams acting, well, like Jason Williams.

In the third quarter of a 112-88 loss at Dallas, Williams began cussing Brendan Brown, Hubie's son, who was the assistant in charge of offensive sets. Hubie Brown said afterward that the incident had "been addressed."

Still, it left Brown wondering if he had the full support of the team as the previous season, when the Grizzlies made their first magical playoff run.

And then there was Brown's health. "Once we started the season, I've had things come up. … Your body gives you a warning sign," Brown said at his hour-long farewell press conference. Brown simply didn't have the energy anymore to coach the way he wanted, agonizing over every detail, sweating out every possession of game. "I need on a daily basis an energy, a stamina and also a spirit. They are the things that drive me into the passion you have for your game. You've got to have that spirit to give you the passion daily. One day you wake up and you don't have that. That's when you understand it's time to walk."

Brown's sudden departure hit his team hard. It was a like a father saying goodbye to his children, and it was emotional when Brown broke the news on the team plane as they sat on the runway Thanksgiving night, preparing to depart to Minnesota.

"I told them it was a fun time for me; and it was an educational thing for me to learn what I could accomplish at this age," Brown said. "I said, 'You guys re-invented me in what I did way back when.' My biggest regret is that I didn't meet them when I was in my 40s and 50s, because I had more to give than I do now. [Back then], I was more alert, more

Hubie Brown gives his acceptance speech upon his induction to the Naismith Basketball Hall of Fame in '05. © 2004 NBA Entertainment. Photo by Joe Murphy

astute, more observant; and I saw more. I apologized to them because I met them too late in my life."

No apologies were needed, according to Grizzlies players.

"Hubie always incorporated life into basketball," then-Griz guard Earl Watson said. "The only other person I knew who did that was [former UCLA coach] John Wooden."

A red-eyed, emotional Jerry West could barely function when Brown told him he was quitting for health concerns and loss of spirit.

"My working relationship with Hubie was second-to-none," West said. "He was my boss, to be honest with you. Whatever he wanted to do, we let him do. I always felt I knew a lot about basketball and understood the nuances of the game. But I can truly tell you: this has been one of the most unique experiences of my life, to work with a man of this caliber and this integrity. It's something I'll cherish when I'm long gone from this league."

It was doubly tough for Brown to walk away. He had come to the bench after 15 years in television, and now he was leaving again after doing the impossible—guiding one of the worst franchises in NBA history to its first-ever playoff berth.

"We could feel you—we could feel the city," Brown said. "Last year was one of the greatest accomplishments in my life, because of the love affair this city had with my kids. You can't do what they did without that 12,000 to 15,000 pulling them through.

"I want to thank the people for your faith in my team, and how you accepted my family. It's really warm walking around in this city."

When Brown's press conference ended after an hour of vintage Hubie, he shook the hand of every media member. Less than a month later, Brown became the lead NBA analyst on ABC; and several months after that, he was elected to the Naismith Basketball Hall of Fame.

9

THE VOICE

THE PERSONABLE MR. POIER

Some people, no matter how bad a day you're having, make you feel good the moment you see them. Long-time Grizzlies radio and television broadcaster Don Poier, who died of an undetected heart condition at a far-too-young age of 53 in Denver in January 2005, was one such person. I heard Don before I met Don. I heard him on the first Grizzlies radio broadcast. It took me about 10 minutes to realize he was one of the best play-by-play announcers I'd ever heard, and certainly the best this city has ever heard.

Listen to Don for just a couple of minutes, and he could entertain you, educate you, and give you the sense he was sitting next to you. That's what great play-by-play announcers do, and he did it in an honest, professional way that pulled no punches. He and analyst Sean Tuohy were a perfect radio fit. Tuohy has a dry sense of humor, and they played off each other. From Day One, they sounded as if they had been broadcast partners for years.

Knowing that I extensively cover SEC football, we talked about the SEC season. Don was an old Pac-10 guy, and he had done regional football and basketball telecasts.

"I gotta tell ya, I'm getting into this SEC football," Don said with a smile. "The teams, the full stadiums, everyone gets beat, no one is safe. ... It's great."

That smile was the best part about Don, as well as his laugh, and his ability to brighten everyone around him. Borrowing a bit of a lyric from the Beatles, Don, for so many years when the franchise was in Vancouver, took a sad team and made it better.

When the Griz do finally win a playoff game, there's no doubt that Don will be watching—and smiling, knowing for the longest time, he'd been on the greatest ride of his life.

I still miss him, and so does everyone who worked with him.

SEAN TUOHY

GRIZZLIES RADIO ANALYST

"I signed my [radio] contract in the stands before the first preseason game, then sat down with Don. Since this was the first NBA game I'd ever done, I told Don I'd listen for the first 10 minutes, get a feel for the game, get a feel for Don's flow. Don says, 'Great idea.'

"So, on the first play Lorenzen [Wright] hits a big shot, The Pyramid goes crazy, Don starts screaming and then he turns to me and says, 'What do you think about that?' I said, 'That was the fastest 10 minutes of my life.'

"He knew everything about pro basketball and I knew very little. I was a slug he carried around for a while. I didn't have anywhere near the talent he had, but he made it work.

"Don was one of the few people I've ever met that was doing exactly what he wanted to do, and he was great at it. He'd tell me several times a day, 'There are 30 of these jobs in the NBA, only 30 jobs like this, and can you believe I got one of them?' If you were ever mad around him, you were stupid because you were going to be the odd man out.

"When you're on the radio, you don't really hear yourself, so you don't know if it was good or bad. But Don was at his best on radio. Even my wife, who hates just about everything I do, told me right away in the beginning that we actually sounded okay. That's when I knew Don was good.

"Don just hated referees. One night in The Pyramid during a timeout with [referee] Ken Mauer standing in front of us, Don is on the air talking very loudly and he's just ripping the officials. Mauer turns around and looks at Don, and Don just keeps on ripping. I tell Don on the air, 'If you keep talking and you get thrown out, we're going to dead air, because I'm not doing play-by-play.' Don really disliked Violet Palmer [the only woman NBA referee]. It wasn't a man-woman thing, he just didn't like her as an official and the fact she was a woman made it easier. This year ['05-'06] when we walked into the arena in Phoenix and I saw Violet Palmer was going to officiate, I said, 'Praise God that Don is not here.' Turns out she was an alternate that night.

"I remember in our first year, he called some referee a 'schmuck.' I said, 'Don, I don't think you can call that guy a schmuck on the air.' Don says, 'He's a schmuck!' I said, 'I don't think you can say that word on the air that you've already used twice.'

"That first year in Memphis, the franchise decided not to send me on the road. So Don did all the road games by himself. So we had a thing on the air after he'd come home off the road where he'd say, 'I've missed you. Where have you been?' And I'd say, 'I kept showing up here to the arena but nobody was here.' That first year, I don't think we won any road games and that had to be tough to call. But the year we won 50 and went to the playoffs for the first time, he'd often tell me, 'You need to enjoy this. This may not happen again. I've been on the other side of it.'"

ANDY DOLICH

GRIZZLIES PRESIDENT OF BUSINESS OPERATIONS

When the franchise was in the planning stages of making the move from Vancouver to Memphis in the spring of 2001, Dolich began formulating a list of employees he wanted to bring south.

"Don was the first person I thought about when we were planning to move the franchise from Vancouver to Memphis," Dolich said. "We were overjoyed when he and Barb said, 'Yeah, that sounds like a grand adventure.' Don was somebody who absolutely got as much out of life as possible.

"Don was the true north of this franchise. From Day One, he had communicated the ups and downs—mostly the downs—with grace, humor, and enthusiasm. He always brought his 'A' game to the microphone when sometimes those around him didn't do that. For those who have always followed the Grizzlies, you know that wasn't always an easy thing to do. There were concerns of someone coming into a totally new market, but I told everyone they would love Don. And that's what happened. Don made you feel he was sitting next to you, telling you what was going on in the game."

MICHAEL CAGE
GRIZZLIES TELEVISION ANALYST

"Don was the master, and I was the apprentice. I had skills, but no experience. But Don never made me feel like a rookie. He knew how to bring out my knowledge and experience as a player. We shared a bond, and when I lost him, it was one of the toughest things I've ever had to deal with. When Don passed, I had a low flame burning. It was very tough on all of us for a while. But Pete [Pranica, Poier's replacement on television] re-lit that flame, and I know Don would tell us that the show must go on."

PETE PRANICA
GRIZZLIES TELEVISION ANNOUNCER

"Don and I were kindred souls with our [broadcasting] approaches. We weren't going to get into coaching, but we wanted to bring the fans on the court between the lines. And we wanted to do it with energy and passion that translated to the viewers and listeners. We wanted fans to realize that this game, with the world's greatest athletes, is pretty amazing."

STEVE DANIEL
GRIZZLIES DIRECTOR OF TEAM OPERATIONS

"Don was the finest and kindest man I've ever met in radio and television. I knew him for 10 years, and I never heard anyone say a single unkind word about that man. With he and his wife, Barb, it was all about what they could do for other people. I spent a lot of holidays at his house, as did [trainer] Scott McCullough. The last time I talked to Don, he said he wanted to work for the Grizzlies forever."

MIKE GOLUB
GRIZZLIES VICE-PRESIDENT OF BUSINESS

"You want the listener to feel like they're sitting down with friends they know they can trust and believe. When people listened to Don and Sean, it's like two guys hanging out and chatting about the game they're watching, but it just happens to be a radio broadcast."

PAU GASOL

"Don was always a great person, he and I always had fun when he was interviewing me. He was 100 percent dedicated to his job, and he was great at it. It was always fun to be around him. Everything I did with him, he was always very human and down to earth. He had a passion for his job, the community, and this team. He was very close to the team. I admired him a lot. He was a great communicator, a great announcer, and a great person."

MIKE MILLER

"He was one of the best announcers I had ever heard. He had a love for what he did. He was with this team from the very beginning here in Memphis, and even before that, and he always cared about what we did. He was a big part of our franchise. He did everything he could always to promote this franchise."

SHANE BATTIER

"Don was truly one of the most genuinely optimistic people you'll ever meet. No matter how bad we were, he always had good things to say about us, and it took a genuinely optimistic person to do that. When we were a really bad team, he had the hardest job of all, because he had to talk about us. But he made us feel good, and made us feel like we were growing."

STROMILE SWIFT

"I'll always remember hearing his voice in the background during our games, including when I was in Vancouver with him. It was always fun hearing his voice during our games or when I was playing video games."

BONZI WELLS

"He was a very important part of our family. To lose someone of that magnitude is a big loss. He was a big ingredient of our family. I only first met him when I came [to Memphis], but he was a great guy. From the first day I got [to Memphis], he embraced me and my family."

RYAN HUMPHREY

"Don was the type of guy who always had a positive attitude. He was always friendly. If he ever saw that you were having a bad day, he'd come over and encourage you, ask about your family … just a caring person."

LORENZEN WRIGHT

"He was more than a part of this team. Every time a record was broken, he'd say, 'I was here for that.'"

LIONEL HOLLINS

GRIZ ASSISTANT COACH

"I can remember in Vancouver when we were really bad. Don would try to put a positive spin on the games during the postgame shows. He tried to keep people interested regardless of what happened. He was perfect to be the voice of the Grizzlies."

POIER-ISMS

Through the years, Poier developed catchphrases unique to his broadcasts.

Rainmaker: A three-pointer.

A Bible and a banjo: Not even these two things would help the struggling defender.

Like bees on bacon: Describing a team's suffocating defense.

Can-opener jam: A slam dunk thrown down with vigor.

Big ol' pile of meat: Big forwards and centers.

IN THE BEGINNING

One thing that certainly helped Poier in his broadcasting was his background as an athlete in Washington. After playing basketball for one year on the freshman team at Washington State, Poier transferred to Pacific Lutheran, where he played defensive end in 1972-73. He graduated in 1974, and those who knew him felt broadcasting was his calling.

Seattle sports columnist Art Thiel, who was two years behind Poier at PLU, never forgot Poier's baritone voice. Said Thiel, "It almost made your chest vibrate. It was clear he had the pipes for doing something in broadcasting."

Poier spent more than 20 years as a regional announcer on Pac-10 Conference football and basketball telecasts. In August of 1995, Poier's company was preparing for his syndicated Pac-10 Conference television show serving the entire West Coast. It was the pregame show to ABC's Pac-10 *Game of the Week*, and it was entering its eighth season. That same month, Poier got a call from his agent. The new NBA franchise in Vancouver, Canada, was looking for a "Voice of the Grizzlies."

It appealed to Poier, because it was one job instead of stringing several together. And there was something else about the Grizzlies job that tweaked his interest.

"Why not be part of something brand new?" Poier said. "Why not start at ground zero and watch a team grow into a respected, winning franchise?"

Poier made the move—and moved again when the Grizzlies moved from Vancouver to Memphis. The second move may have been tougher than the first.

"After 25 years of broadcasting on the West Coast, my wife, Barb, and I were confronted with our first major move," Poier recalled after a couple of years in Memphis. "It meant leaving kids, grandkids, and friends. Plus, how would we be accepted? I came with the credibility of being the original announcer, but would fans take to my style? Would they take to the Grizzlies at all?"

Poier missed just four Grizzlies games during his decade-long tenure—the last two coming in December 2004, when he attended the college graduation of one of his daughters.

The Grizzlies, as his wife, Barb said, "were his life for 10 years." Usually when you saw Don, you saw Barb. She loved his job as much as he did, because one of the perks was a long off-season in which the Poiers traveled the country in their 36-foot RV, which Don described as "our land yacht." They'd often head out west to see some of their eight children and 10 grandchildren.

Such a break always helped Poier rev his engines for another season. Grizzlies fans certainly appreciated Poier. Before he switched from the primary radio voice of the team to the television side, numerous fans would tell him they liked to turn down the television audio and listen to his radio play-by-play.

"That's the highest compliment you can get," Poier once said. "My style is enthusiasm with honesty. I go with emotion and description more than clichés."

Don Poier was the real deal. It came through in every one of his broadcasts.

HE'LL ALWAYS BE A GRIZZLY

The Grizzlies made sure that Poier will never be forgotten. They put the spirit of Poier in the FedExForum media center—re-named The Don Poier Media Center—where his pictures and his sayings grace the walls.

The center has photos and memorabilia honoring Poier for his contributions to the Grizzlies and the community. It's a great tribute to a fine man, his lovely wife, Barbara, and his three daughters, four stepdaughters, and stepson.

At the dedication of the room, Griz majority owner Michael Heisley noted Poier's key role in helping the franchise move from Vancouver to Memphis.

"He became the friendly face of the Memphis Grizzlies," Heisley said. "He was hugely responsible for the universal acceptance we achieved in this city."

10

THE WRIGHT STUFF

AFTER MIDNIGHT

As midnight passed with the 2001 NBA draft less than 24 hours away, Lorenzen Wright got the best news of his pro career. He learned from family members watching ESPN that he'd just been traded from the Hawks to the Grizzlies along with starting point guard Brevin Knight for forward Abdur-Rahim. The Grizzlies also got the Hawks' No. 3 pick overall, which became Pau Gasol.

"Hands down, this is the best day of my life," said Wright while shopping for a larger house in Memphis just hours after learning of the trade. "Everyone in my family is happy. I'm so blessed. When I played in California [for the Clippers], it was great place. And then moving to Atlanta was like moving to my home team because Atlanta was the closest city to Memphis that had a NBA team. When I heard the Grizzlies were coming to Memphis, I was just happy with the fact that I'd get to come home to Memphis with the Hawks and play here twice a year.

"I've never thought I'd have a chance to have my cake and eat it, too. The Grizzlies had wanted me before when they were in Vancouver. But I didn't want to go there for the same reasons a lot of players didn't—it's too far away and the taxes are too high. I always knew, though, that they liked me."

THE HEART OF A LION

It's true that Wright has never had the size of a typical NBA center. He's just 6-feet-11 and around 250 pounds. But never mention to Wright that he's undersized. He has never backed down from anyone.

"When Lorenzen has that swagger, and he's woofin', we have an inside presence," former Griz forward Shane Battier said.

Wright, who had the fiercest scowl on the team before becoming a free agent in the summer of '06, comes by his intensity honestly. His father, Herb, played the same way when he hit the boards in college for Shelby State and Ole Miss, and he trained his son to play the same way. In the summer, Lorenzen has trained under Herb's supervision since eighth grade; and just as when he started, it's no summer vacation.

"My Dad is very intense, just like his dad was intense," Wright said. "People always tell me, 'I bet you look forward to the end of the season.' The season is just playing games. It's nothing compared to training with my Dad in the off-season. I never think anything in a season is harder than running around a lake or running through sand dunes in the summer. But it's that intensity, that focus, that has helped me. You've got to concentrate in this game, even when you come off the bench.

"The only problem I have is people thinking I can't play the position because they think I'm undersized. If somebody is bigger than me, I feel I can make that up with intensity and heart."

Wright's 10-year NBA career through the '06 season may have surprised some people, but he has lasted a long time due to his desire and his savvy. He knows the tricks of being a NBA center. It could be a push here, a grab there, or a forearm on the back, or hooking a defender where the referee can't see it.

"I'll do something in practice and the rookies say, 'You can't do that,'" Wright said. "I say, 'Hey, Rook, if the referees don't see it, don't tell me what I can't do.'"

Former Griz center Lorenzen Wright knew how to raise everyone's intensity level.
© 2005 NBA Entertainment. Photo by Joe Murphy

ONE FOR THE SON

The March 1, 2004, game at San Antonio was a battle, but the Grizzlies clawed back to trail by a point in the final seconds. So it figured that a sheer hustle play was going to win the game for the Griz, and Wright was just the man to provide it. He grabbed an offensive rebound and jammed it back in the basket with 19 seconds left for the 81-80 victory.

"I just wanted to be persistent," Wright said. "I wanted to get after the loose ball and get the rebound. The ball ended up in my hands and I went back up strong. I've never hit a game-winning shot before in the NBA. My son liked it. He's still talking about it."

WRIGHT'S TOUGHEST GAME

A game on March 16, 2003, for the Grizzlies seemed like any other night at the office. But it wasn't certainly for Wright.

It was his first game back since his 11-month-old daughter Sierra died of undetermined circumstances on March 1. Wright's performance of 21 points and eight rebounds in 24 minutes in a 124-92 win over the Hawks was nothing short of remarkable.

"There were so many emotions for me," said Wright, who entered and exited the game to heartfelt standing ovations. "I didn't want to come in, rush, and start messing up. [Grizzlies coach] Hubie [Brown] told me to take my time, and let the game come to me."

THE OLD SOFT SHOE

In early February of the '04-'05 season, Wright finally retired the same Nike shoe style he had been wearing for three seasons, which was stunning, since NBA players get free shoes and change styles more than they change underwear.

Wright busted out his new Nikes against the Suns, finally putting his old Nikes on the shelf … sort of. "I had them brought to the bench in case I needed to change back to them during the game," Wright said.

What was unusual about Wright's old shoes—let's call them Lorenzen Wrights—was that they were so out of style, they were selling for $19.99 on eastbay.com, a great place to buy the latest and not-so-latest in athletic footwear. When our guy Lorenzen was informed you could pick up a pair of Lorenzen Wrights for a $20, he started laughing.

"I keep asking Nike for them because they felt good on my feet," he said. "That's all that matters to me. They felt good on my feet. I don't care if they are pretty."

Wright had tried his newest pair of Nikes before, but didn't like them.

"I tried them in practice one day, and I thought they might work, maybe it was time for a change," Wright said. "I wore them in the first half of the next game and almost twisted my ankle in them. That was it. I went in at halftime and changed back to my old shoes. But I went back and asked Nike to get me a pair at a smaller size."

Lorenzen is now happy with his new shoes. Whatever happened to his old kicks?

"They are still in my locker if I need them," he said. "They won't be too far away."

FIND A NEW SPEAKER

When the Grizzlies were planning their pregame ceremonies for the first-ever regular-season game in the new FedExForum to start the '04-'05 season, it was natural that Wright was to be the team's representative to speak to the fans. After all, he starred at the University of Memphis and was the team's hometown link.

But Milwaukee center Zaza Pachulia took Wright off the bill. A few days before the season opener, in an exhibition, Pachulia elbowed Wright twice in the face before Wright shoved him. Officials only saw the shove, and Wright was ejected from the game. The ejection carried a one-game suspension, that being the season opener. So much for Wright's opening-night words of wisdom.

"I was supposed to speak," said a glum Wright.

SON, IT'S ABOUT THE SKYHOOK —NOT THE NO-LOOK

Wright had dreams as a teenager of being the next Magic Johnson, the ball-handling whiz of the Lakers' "Showtime" NBA championship teams of the 1980s. Even as Wright kept growing to the size of a center, he never lost that hunger to lead the fast break.

"Every big guy wanted to be Magic, dribbling and throwing no-look passes," Wright said. "Of course, after I threw a couple of no-looks, my Daddy saw me. That was the end of my no-look passing. So I looked at some things that center did, like [the Lakers'] Kareem Abdul-Jabbar. He had that skyhook, and the hook shot was one of the first shots I learned."

THIS ONE'S FOR YOU, DEAN

The Wrights—Lorenzen and Herb—conducted their off-season training in Memphis at Dean Lotz Personal Fitness.

When Herb wasn't around, it was Dean or Dean's son, Beau, who pushed Lorenzen. Dean, a former strength coach at the University of Memphis, had an almost-magical touch on training athletes. Big-name pros flocked to him, knowing he could make them stronger and faster in a matter of weeks.

When Wright entered the NBA in 1996, he discovered weightlifting needed to be a year-round proposition. It didn't take him long to discover "… all the pushing and tugging made [the NBA] a dirty game," he said.

Dean Lotz and assistant, Harry Schuh, used to marvel at Wright's year-by-year physical development.

"We were looking at some pictures of Lorenzen when he was a rookie," Schuh said. "He had skinny arms. He doesn't have those anymore. He's solid, especially in his thighs and rear."

In December 2004, while raking leaves in his yard, Dean Lotz suffered a heart attack and died. All his clients took the news hard, especially Wright. He immediately wrote a tribute on one of his basketball shoes, and he wore them in several games.

"Dean was the first person to ever put a weight in my hand," said Wright, who wrote "Dean Lotz, R.I.P." on one of his Nikes. "I've worked out with him since I was 16 years old. He was a great guy, a class guy. I never saw Dean ever get mad or curse or do anything wrong. I loved him, and I'll miss him."

THE CONTRACT DISPUTE

In the summer of '05, with a year remaining on his contract, Wright uncharacteristically called a press conference and demanded a trade because the Grizzlies refused to discuss a contract extension with him.

"I would love for the Grizzlies to sign me, and I'd be a Grizzly for the rest of my life," Wright said. "But when we went to them about signing an extension, they didn't give me a chance to say what I wanted. They just said, 'We're cutting costs, and we're not doing any business deals.' I wanted the chance to say, 'Will you give me five dollars a day?' But they said, 'We're not doing anything. We're not going to do it now. We're not going to do it in six months. We'll talk after this season.'"

When word of Wright's contract dispute hit the media, the most upset people were the players and the parents of the players of the YOMCA 10-and-under AAU team, which is funded and coached by Wright—parents like LaQuitha Williams.

"My son [Kytrel] told me he'd go talk to [Griz president] Jerry West himself, that he'd tell him, 'Don't take my coach away, Mr. West,'" Williams said. "He'd said he'd do anything to keep Lorenzen here."

Williams said she didn't understand why the Grizzlies won't even negotiate with Wright, who has been the local face tied to the franchise since it moved to Memphis from Vancouver in the summer of 2001.

"Lorenzen is a very important part of the community, and he does more than the average NBA player for this community," Williams said. "[Plus], he's an excellent ballplayer. He's like the Elvis of basketball in our city. He's being treated unfairly."

Wright assured his players and the parents that he'd always coach the team, no matter what happens after the 2005-06 season.

"Lorenzen told everyone that 'No matter what happens, if I'm playing here or anywhere else, I'm always going to live here in the off-season and coach this team,'" said Heather Moorman, whose son, Evan, plays for Wright.

Griz president Jerry West didn't comment when Wright blasted away in his June press conference. But he addressed the issue when the team reported for training camp in October.

"Somebody said, 'Are you upset with Lorenzen?'" West said. "Absolutely not. That's what he chose to do, but it doesn't bother me."

Wright said he had prayed on the issue and believed that the Grizzlies would be fair with him at the end of the season when his contract expired.

"You have to hold a man to his word," Wright said. "They say they'll negotiate fairly, so I believe them. I'm not mad at the owner, at Jerry West, at Coach, or anybody because they're doing their jobs, too. I'd like to think that they understood where I was coming from."

BEING A TEAM PLAYER

The one thing Wright's father instilled in his son, "The bottom line is winning. Put aside personal goals, and hopes; and win." That's why Wright couldn't understand the discontentment from teammates Jason Williams and Bonzi Wells late in the '04-'05 season, when the Grizzlies were battling to hold on to a playoff spot.

If Williams wasn't screaming at his coach about playing time, Wells was throwing his headband and wristbands in the stands in disgust when getting pulled from a game.

"Our team would be playing great, our players [would be] knocking down their shots and everybody [would be] up and clapping, except for a couple of guys," Wright said. "I couldn't understand that."

During the '05-'06 season, Wright lost his starting job. Instead of being a whiny veteran he supported new starter, Jake Tsakalidis, and gave solid effort off the bench.

In the final months of the season, Wright played some of his best basketball as a pro. He discovered some advantages of being a bench player.

"I'm able to have a different mind-set," Wright said. "When I start, I'm more of a defensive player. Coming off the bench [with more fouls to give], I'm able to be more reckless, which is the way I like to play. I can score more and do other things in the game besides just play defense."

Griz coach Mike Fratello appreciated Wright's professionalism, particularly in light of his preseason contract dispute, saying, "I always root for him to do really well."

DON'T BUG ME

Want to know Wright's weakness? Try roaches.

Before one of the Grizzlies' practices in Dallas for the '05-'06 play offs, Wright was talking with the media when a roach scurried across the court near his feet.

Wright danced like a man dodging bullets as the roach ran in circles.

Jarvis Greer, a television sportscaster from WMC-TV in Memphis, put Wright at ease. Showing killer instinct, Greer stomped on the roach.

STAY JUST A LITTLE BIT LONGER

When the Grizzlies were swept in the '05-'06 playoffs by the Mavericks, extending the Griz playoff record to 0-12, the reality for Wright was his career with the Griz might be over. Wright officially became a free agent after the 26-point loss to the Mavs in Game 4.

"It has been great being with this franchise from the beginning," Wright said. "Coming from where we were, as down as we were, and becoming a playoff team, I just hope I have an opportunity to be here when we get our first playoff win."

Wright said he had peace of mind that his situation would be resolved.

"I struggled with it early in the season, beat myself over the head with it," Wright said. "Now I just want to come out next year, think just about basketball, and have fun. If they [the Grizzlies' management] are fair with me, I want to be back here next year. If they want to do a sign-and-trade or whatever, I'll be very cooperative. I've always been very professional with this organization, and I don't plan on changing that. If they can help me or if I can help them, I'll do it."

Wright said the one thing he wanted to be remembered for was his intensity.

"I always play hard," he said. "Sometimes, the minutes I got weren't indicative of the player I wanted to be, but I always gave 110 percent. I've had a great time here. I don't want it to end."

11

IT'S A MEMPHIS THING

TIME TO PARTY

On the last day of June 2001, just two days after the NBA approved the move of the Grizzlies to Memphis, fans packed Peabody Place for a huge celebration that featured majority owner Michael Heisley beaming like a proud father.

"I always felt, when I chose Memphis, that the enthusiasm would be here," Heisley said. "The thing that lets you know this is a basketball city is when you talk to fans here, they really know basketball. I think that's one of the situations we're going to have here over the situation in Vancouver."

When hometown-product Lorenzen Wright modeled a Grizzlies jersey, the standing-room-only crowd at Peabody Place erupted.

"I'd never seen anything like this in Memphis before," Wright said that day. "When I was handed that jersey, it was like I felt when I was a kid and I got my very first jersey. I felt like I was starting all over again."

No one was more pumped than Memphis mayor Willie Herenton, who screamed to the crowd, "Memphis, doesn't it feel good? NBA MEMPHIS!"

Herenton may have gotten a bit carried away when he said, "We're going to build a first-class arena, and in a couple of years, we're going to be in the NBA Finals, and then we're going to win the championship!"

Below Herenton, in the front row, Griz coach Sidney Lowe appeared as though he was in shock. "Oh, man, the shoulders are getting heavy," he said. "This is unbelievable."

MOVING IN

In the first two weeks of July 2001, the Griz set up business operations on the 10th floor of the AutoZone Annex.

"We look like a duck paddling in a pond," said Andy Dolich, the team's president of business operations during that hectic month. "On the surface, it looks calm. But underneath the surface ... "

Dolich said he was getting used to fighting the odds. When Michael Heisley bought the team the previous summer in Vancouver, the business operation got a late start on promoting the upcoming season.

"We started late last year, but this year is going to be a real sprint," Dolich said. "When we took over in Vancouver, we had some existing infrastructure. We've got to set up new infrastructure."

Even with 7,500 deposits on season tickets, Dolich wasn't taking anything for granted. The team planned to transfer 15 front-office employees from Vancouver and hire about 50 to 60 people.

"We're at the point where we might put people to work 15 minutes after we get them," Dolich said.

THE BEAR FACTS

Late in their first season of 2001-02, the Grizzlies announced they weren't going to change their nickname.

"We're definitely the Grizzlies; we are, and we will be the Grizzlies," Dolich said.

There had been talk when the team moved from Vancouver that the nickname would be changed to "Express" because of the FedEx sponsorship of the proposed new arena.

"We looked very seriously at a name change, whether we tied it to Memphis music, food, or the river," Dolich said. "Some people thought we might use Showboats [the nickname of Memphis' defunct USFL team], but that was never going to happen."

Through fan surveys, formal and informal, Dolich discovered Memphis fans liked the nickname Grizzlies.

"In conversations that we had with people and in focus groups, we were frankly surprised that people rated the name so highly," Dolich said. "Originally, we were under the assumption we'd definitely have a name change and a logo change. But the nickname Grizzlies has way above a 70-percent approval rating in fan surveys, and there isn't another name that comes close. We'd be crazy to change the name. It's what the consumers want. People like talking about 'The Griz.'"

MORE THEMES THAN A PROM

From year to year, pro teams have one central promotional theme to push season tickets and keep a team in the public's eye. The Grizzlies are no different, but their "Round Town" theme during their second season in Memphis in '02-'03 may have been their best-selling campaign.

The reason was a series of commercials created by Memphis ad agency Conaway Brown. The television spots featured everything from Pau Gasol and Shane Battier eating ribs at Corky's; to Lorenzen Wright explaining a Memphis map to rookie Drew Gooden; to Jason Williams whipping a garbage bag behind his back into a garbage truck; to Jerry West carefully helping a grocery store shopper select fruit. While all the commercials were catchy, none was funnier than Gasol trying to teach Battier several words of Spanish while munching on ribs. When Gasol gasps after biting a spicy rib, Battier looks directly into the camera, and says with much gusto, "Caliente!"

"I guess I just do everything with a lot of passion," Battier explained.

MY TOWN, MY TEAM

No one was prouder of the team's first season in Memphis than center Lorenzen Wright, who said he always dreamed as a teenager that the city would have an NBA team one day.

"I knew a team here would work," Wright said at the end of the first season in Memphis. "When I played for Atlanta, and we played the

Knicks, the arena would be full of Knicks fans. Here in Memphis, our fans are our fans. The only things we're missing now are wins."

SPANNING THE REGION

Leeta Stevens is a housewife, mother, and substitute teacher in Portageville, Missouri. But over the past couple of years, she has been the Grizzlies' Pied Piper of Portageville, becoming exactly the type of regional fan the Grizzlies are seeking.

She first recruited six high school students, friends of her children, to go to a Griz game three years ago. Word spread that going to an NBA game was blast, and the next year that group grew to 40. Finally during the 2003-04 season, Stevens got so many people that she had to get a school bus to drive the 103 miles south to Memphis.

"We only have 3,500 people in our town, and I'd rather have the kids with us, going to an event that's good wholesome, family entertainment," said Stevens, who organizes groups two to three times a year for a trek to Memphis. "You see a lot of kids now at school wearing Grizzlies T-shirts and caps."

Such a statement is what the Grizzlies want to hear as they try to sink their claws into the regional market extending in at least a two-hour, 150-mile radius of Memphis in every direction.

"We understood from Day One that, if we didn't build a regional franchise, that we were going to be challenged in the future," Dolich said. "Our local fan base is very loyal, so we need to do another 10 to 17 percent from the regional market. We want to see faces we haven't seen before. Loyalties in this marketplace are deeply seeded and not easily generated. People here aren't just going to jump on a bandwagon because somebody says you should jump on a bandwagon."

CAN YOU FEEL THE LOVE?

Once Jerry West, then Hubie Brown, arrived to form the foundation of a franchise serious about winning, the Memphis fans were overwhelmingly appreciative.

Majority owner Michael Heisley recalled the final home game of the '02-'03 season, in which the Grizzlies won a then-franchise-record 28 games. As Heisley walked from his mid-court seat at halftime, fan after fan thanked Heisley for bringing the team to Memphis from Vancouver.

"I feel like a guy walking down the street in a blizzard, and someone has opened a door and said, 'Come on in,'" Heisley said. "I came in, and it was Memphis. People keep saying what I've done for Memphis. It's more like what Memphis has done for me. It has been fantastic. I'm very happy."

THE FAST TRACK TO SUCCESS

When the Grizzlies made the playoffs for the first time in '03-'04, it stirred the emotions of Gayle Rose, who was part of the original pursuit team trying to attract an NBA franchise to Memphis.

"It's just breathtaking because, in many ways, this city is still adjusting to the fact we have an NBA team," said Rose a day after the Grizzlies clinched their first-ever playoff berth on March 28, 2004. "Having success this fast, considering where we came from, is just unexpected."

The team that moved to Memphis could have been Charlotte if Griz owner Michael Heisley hadn't stepped boldly into the relocation fray.

"We just wanted a team, and there wasn't a lot of thought about it," Rose said. "We didn't say, 'Let's get a good one.' We had to get what might be available. We spent a lot of time talking to the Hornets, and we thought they might be the team. They were really good at the time. The Grizzlies popped up on the screen late in the relocation game."

Rose said that one reason Memphis fell in love with the Grizzlies, when Hubie Brown took over as coach early in the second season of the franchise after the move from Vancouver, was Brown's 10-man rotation. It promoted team play, passing, unselfishness— all the things that basketball is supposed to embody.

"While we learned as a city to love individual players," Rose said, "the Grizzlies taught us there's value in the strength of teamwork. They've proved to the rest of the United States that you necessarily don't need a big star to win."

NEW LOOK AND NEW DIGS

Since the early 1990s in the NBA, the way to sell an image makeover of your team is to open a new arena, get a new logo, change colors, and order a uniform re-design.

Call it "Marketing Eyes for the NBA Guys."

Houston did it in '03-'04 with the opening of the Toyota Center. Dallas took the plunge in '01 when the Mavs moved into the American Airlines Center. Golden State's new logo appeared in '97 when the Warriors began playing in their new digs in Oakland. Phoenix's move in '92 to America West prompted a logo change. It was the same with the Grizzlies as they moved into the FedExForum for the 2004-05 season. The new logo and sharp colors of Memphis Midnight, Beale Street Blue, Smoke Blue, and Grizzlies Gold were a big hit.

"Our logo design that won was liked by everyone who saw it and who had input in the selection process," said Mike Golub, former Grizzlies vice-president of business operations. "It reflected the region and the fans of Memphis. We wanted a logo and colors that would look good on our court at FedExForum, then on our uniform. Something clean and something timeless."

When the Grizzlies moved to Memphis from Vancouver in 2001, the original plan was to forge a completely new identity—change the nickname, the colors, and the logo. But through fan surveys, the franchise discovered Memphis fans identified with the nickname.

The logo and the colors were another matter.

Marla Taner, the Grizzlies' senior director of marketing communication, said the original logo and colors of red, teal, black and white were designed and chosen by the NBA.

"If you looked at our logo, it was this huge teal Grizzlies and the city, whether it was Vancouver or Memphis, in small letters," Taner said. "You see the Grizzlies rather than the city."

There was no doubt that some players disliked the Grizzlies' color scheme, which in the Vancouver days included an all-teal uniform.

"I hated those uniforms—they were awful," said Sacramento guard Mike Bibby, who played for the Grizzlies from 1998 to 2001.

COACHING FROM THE UPPER DECK

At NBA games, arenas are separated into almost two different countries.

There are the lower level seats that go for $75 and more, many of which are owned by corporations. Many of the fans in the lower level concentrate more on yelling at the officials than anything else. But if you go sit in the upper deck, where tickets are more affordable, you'll find the blue-collar fan. His concern is coaching the various Grizzlies who may not be playing up to the par.

A case in point happened during a game against the Utah Jazz in January '06. A Grizzlies fan was clearly exasperated with Griz forward Pau Gasol's maddening habit of holding the ball too long in the post before settling for a fadeaway jumper or passing back out to the guard.

After Gasol did this several times, he got the ball again. At that point, the angry fan screamed in a voice that could be heard at courtside, "TAKE THE BALL TO THE BASKET, PAU!"

At that moment, Gasol head-faked his defender, drove the basket, and scored. Everyone sitting in the section where Gasol's new upper-deck coach was sitting broke out in wild applause. Naturally, the fan threw his hands in the air, acknowledging that, yes, he was a brilliant coach—even if only for a moment.

THE BLING WAS THE THING

There are many headaches when you're the majority owner of any pro team in any sport. So, naturally, when you get a chance to be a little goofy, you take it—as Michael Heisley did before game three of the '05 Western Conference first-round playoff series against the Suns. As the Griz players filtered to the FedExForum floor for a casual pregame shoot-around about two hours before game time, Heisley, wearing a massive diamond earring, greeted them.

No, he didn't get his ear pierced.

"I borrowed this diamond from a jeweler, and he made a special screw-on setting for me," said Heisley, who had two security guards follow him around to guard the diamond, which Heisley said was worth upper-six figures.

Griz guard Bonzi Wells, who always called Heisley "Big Money," was awed by the rock dangling from Heisley's ear.

"That ... is ... huge," said Wells, shaking his head.

12

HELLO, FRATELLO

HIT THE GROUND RUNNING

"Mike Fratello, these are the Grizzlies. Grizzlies, this is your new coach, Mike Fratello. Now go, win."

That's about how quick the introductions were before the Grizzlies' first practice with Mike Fratello and his staff, nearly a week after Hubie Brown resigned on Thanksgiving night 2004.

"It was little tough because we lost our emotional leader [Hubie Brown]," Griz forward Shane Battier said. "But we all came to work with a smile—with good attitudes ready to get after it again."

For Fratello, putting on an NBA coaching shirt, sweatpants, and basketball shoes for the first time in five and a half years was also gratifying. Like his predecessor, Brown, he had thrived as a television analyst, not knowing if he'd ever get another legitimate chance to coach after he was fired in Cleveland in '99 after six seasons. But even though the first few days were a whirlwind for Fratello, he looked like a man ready to get back to teaching and coaching the game he loved.

"This is a very receptive team," Fratello said at his first press conference as Griz coach. "They want to be able to regroup, build from where we are and get ourselves back into the playoff situation. We have enough games [left] to do that, but we have to play better than we've played the last couple of games. They're capable of it. It's a matter of working together on the stuff we're beginning to work on."

Many of the Grizzlies emphasized their relief of having a new coach and staff, led by former Golden State coach Eric Musselman in place. Retained from Brown's former staff were assistant Lionel Hollins, who served as interim coach, and workout coach John Welch.

"It has been tough, because we didn't know if we were going to stick with Coach Hollins, or if we were going to have a new coach, and what kind of coach it would be," Griz forward Pau Gasol said when Fratello was hired. "We were kind of confused."

Dazed, bewildered, disappointed—the Grizzlies ran the gamut of emotions after Brown boarded their charter flight in Memphis on Thanksgiving night and told them prior to departure for a road game at Minnesota that he was quitting.

"It was so sudden, it took us by surprise; and you don't prepare for that," former Griz point guard Earl Watson said. "But it's basketball. You gather yourself and you move on. There's a beginning and ending to everything, and this is a beginning."

There was some familiarity between some of the Grizzlies and their new coaches.

First-year Grizzlies forward Brian Cardinal played for Musselman at Golden State. New assistant Mitchell Anderson was an assistant on former Griz coach Sidney Lowe's staff when the team moved to Memphis in 2001-02, then became a team scout when Brown became coach in November 2002. And not to make the 57-year-old Fratello feel ancient, but, as a kid in the mid-1980s Watson said he remembered watching Fratello coach the Atlanta Hawks.

"I really wasn't old enough to know basketball," Watson said. "But Atlanta had those high flyers like Dominique [Wilkins], Spud Webb, and Doc Rivers. They were fun to watch play."

Mike Fratello has built playoff-caliber teams at each of his three NBA coaching stops. © 2005 NBA Entertainment. Photo by Nikki Boertman

LIVING THE GOOD LIFE WASN'T ENOUGH

If a blueprint existed for spending the latter years of a lifetime in basketball, Fratello had found it:

Earn a lucrative living as an analyst for TNT national telecasts and for the Miami Heat, living in a South Beach condo half the year; first-class travel; eat at the best restaurants; stay at the nicest hotels; visit basketball coaching friends in every NBA stop; work with the best broadcast partners.

At the end of the night, whatever game he worked on television, when the final buzzer sounded, his stomach didn't churn mulling over a tight win or a close loss. His major postgame decision was finding an open restaurant for a late-night dinner and some laughs.

You can't draw up a better job description.

But for a born competitor such as Fratello, five years of being involved with the game, but not being *in* the game, created an emptiness that only his close friends knew existed.

"I had a nice job; I liked what I was doing; and I worked with great people," Fratello said. "But as a coach, you miss preparing a team for an 82-game season, preparing a team for every game situation. You even miss the misery of winning and losing, because it's a job where you wind up beating yourself up a lot when the games are done, even on nights that you win."

Late Thanksgiving afternoon in 2004, the phone rang at Fratello's hotel room in Indianapolis where he was preparing for that night's Pacers-Timberwolves national telecast. On the other end of the line was Grizzlies president Jerry West, who was about to make Fratello—thankfully ... finally—miserable.

WHERE DID HE GO?

Until West broke the emergency glass and hired the 57-year-old former Atlanta and Cleveland coach, Fratello's five-year absence from the sideline was one of the league's great mysteries.

"It's pretty incredible that guy was passed over for jobs for five years," said Heat assistant Ron Rothstein, a former Fratello assistant in Atlanta and Cleveland. "What were front-office people doing during that time?

A lot of people who had the opportunity to hire Mike should be kicking themselves today."

"Honestly, Mike being out of the game [made me] scared that I might not ever get back in the game," said Nuggets coach George Karl, hired by Denver on January 27, 2005, after last coaching in 2002-03 for Milwaukee.

"When a very qualified teacher like Mike Fratello is out of the game for five years, that tells me there are a lot of general managers and owners who maybe aren't qualified to know where quality coaches are," Bulls coach Scott Skiles said.

While working on television, Fratello had flirtations with teams, such as the Clippers and Knicks, where during the '03-'04 season that the New *York Daily News* reported that "an announcement was forthcoming" about Fratello's hiring.

"I wasn't looking for utopia where there was a Shaquille O'Neal, a Kevin Garnett, a Tim Duncan," Fratello said. "The places I had a chance to go to, I felt those people weren't the right match for me, as far as thinking the way I thought on how things needed to be done. I knew every time I said 'no' it might prolong it [becoming a coach again] that much longer."

When West called, though, and told Fratello, "We're having a press conference tomorrow; Hubie's stepping down for health reasons. Would you be interested in talking to us about the job?" Fratello already knew the Grizzlies' situation well. It took a face-to-face meeting with West and four more days of thought before Fratello signed a four-year, $16-million contract.

Brown, who was hired immediately by ABC-TV as an analyst, said that he has rarely missed watching his former team and protégé. He's proud of both.

"It was the perfect job for Michael, and it was the perfect hire by the team," Brown said. "They needed someone with the experience to get it done. They needed someone who has coached different styles of play. It's still a young team, and they needed all of the above. If they were going to step out of the organization, there's nobody better than Michael."

Majority owner Michael Heisley agreed, as he watched Fratello make a seamless transition.

"I'd be liar to say I wasn't concerned, because we were going from a guy who was the league's Coach of the Year [Brown], to someone else," said Heisley near the end of the 2004-05 season. "I've known Mike and admired him, but the job he did for us, particularly when we had so many people injured, was just outstanding. I'm prouder of this team than the one last year that won 50 because of the hardships they faced."

JERSEY DAYS

Fratello was raised in Hackensack, New Jersey, as the only child of Vince and Maria Fratello. His father, an Army veteran, was a boxer—a two-time Golden Gloves winner as an amateur—with more than 60 pro fights to his credit. For many years, his parents ran a luncheonette in downtown Hackensack. It was a great time and place to be a kid. Fratello lived in a neighborhood where a group of guys, led by an older boy named Tony Karcich, always made sure there were games being played or there was a movie to be seen. When one guy went, everyone went.

Karcich—one of the best high school football coaches in New Jersey history with 14 state championships—said Fratello, his longtime buddy, was always in the middle of the action as a three-sport athlete at Hackensack High in baseball, basketball, and football.

"Mike never let size disadvantage bother him, especially in basketball," said Karcich, football coach and athletic director at St. Joseph's Regional High in Montvale, New Jersey. "He had this dirty little trick on defense. If you were much taller than him, and he had no chance to block your shot, he'd get as close to you as he could and jab you in the stomach with a finger or two from his right hand. The refs would never see it because they were looking at Mike's left hand, which was raised trying to block the shot."

Fratello, who got some of his father's competitive genes and some of his mother's feisty personality, never backed down.

"Everything in our neighborhood was a game," Fratello said. "'Who can do this, who can do that, who can get there first' … it was always some kind of challenge. We split up into teams or we'd go to the next town over and challenge somebody."

When Fratello went off to college at Montclair (New Jersey) State with the intent of becoming a high school coach and teacher, he got a call one day from a coach at Fair Lawn High who also happened to be running a summer swim club. It was Hubie Brown. He wanted to hire a lifeguard, and he called Fratello, remembering him as a relentless player against whom he coached, and invited him to play in his summer basketball league. Brown never stopped calling Fratello. When Brown took his first college assistant job at William & Mary and then moved on to Duke, he'd call Fratello, who was still in college to scout opponents. He then brought him to Duke to teach at the summer basketball camp and recommended Fratello for his first college job as freshman coach at Rhode Island in 1970. Brown gave Fratello his first pro coaching job as an assistant with the Hawks in 1978, then as an assistant with the Knicks in 1982, before Fratello began his own full-time NBA head coaching career in 1983 at Atlanta.

"Michael has always been a leader," Brown said. "He had that presence as a high school athlete, and he was a leader of powerhouse football and baseball teams. Once he got into coaching, he became an outstanding teacher. I hired him because of that. I never hired anybody as an assistant who couldn't teach."

BUILDING AN NBA RESUME

Former Fratello assistant Ron Rothstein said that Fratello is blessed with, among other things, an incredible memory.

"There are things that slip your mind or get away, but Mike never forgot things," Rothstein said. "You could bring up a game or something with another organization, and he had a great recall. His preparation was flawless. He always wrote everything down."

Former Grizzlies head coach Sidney Lowe, an assistant under Fratello in Cleveland from 1994-99 after playing for him in Atlanta in 1984-85, said Fratello takes time to learn his players and coaches.

"When I was with him at Cleveland, I had a habit in practice of constantly talking to the defense, communicating with them like I was a player, calling screens and such," Lowe said. "One day at practice, I wasn't feeling well, and I wasn't saying much. Mike gave me a few choice words, like 'What's wrong with you today? Cat got your tongue?' I started laughing because I realized that the guy knows me so well, he knew something was wrong when I wasn't talking."

Players who have played under Fratello swear by him. They rave about his ability to adapt to personnel and situations. When he coached the Hawks, he had a team full of fast-breaking, high-flying talent, led by such stars as Dominique "The Human Highlight Film" Wilkins, Doc Rivers, Spud Webb, and Kevin Willis. In Fratello's seven years there, from 1983 to 1990, his teams averaged 107.7 points and 46.3 wins. There was a four-year stretch where the Hawks annually won 50 or more games.

"Mike was a great coach," said Dominique Wilkins. "He knew that everyone brought a piece of the puzzle to the team. He got everyone to work together. We were all on the same page. Every night, everyone laid it on the line for him."

At Cleveland from 1993 to 1999, Fratello took over a situation that changed drastically from his first season to his third. By year three, his top-five scorers from the first season, including longtime stars Brad Daugherty, Larry Nance, "Hot Rod" Williams, and Mark Price, had retired, sustained career-ending injuries, or had been traded. Fratello's roster became so full of young players and no-names that he had to change offensive style to fit the personnel.

"It was a very delicate situation," Fratello said. "If I just substituted the wrong way with a certain group of players, teams could get a 15-2 run on us. We didn't have the athleticism, the firepower, or the talent to run up and down the floor. You've got to be smart how you play. I didn't say, 'Don't run the basketball.' I said, 'Shot selection … pass the basketball.'"

With a deliberate attack, Cleveland kept going to the playoffs, with such role players as Michael Cage, now the Grizzlies' television analyst, who played two seasons under Fratello from 1994 to 1996. "I watched Mike turn some young underachievers into real pros," Cage said. "He was very flexible. Coaches who aren't confident about what they're doing are inflexible. Mike checked their egos at the door."

Fratello's critics say he was fired after the strike-shortened season of 1998-99 because he had reduced the Cavs to a slow-down team that scored in the high 80s and low 90s. It apparently didn't matter that four of his six teams in Cleveland made the playoffs.

"We had post up guys like [Shawn] Kemp, 'Z' [Zydrunas Ilgauskas], and Vitaly [Potapenko] who were our bread and butter," said Charlotte guard Brevin Knight, a former Grizzly who broke into the league as a rookie starter with the Cavs under Fratello in 1997-98. "What was going to make us win was throw the ball to the post. We didn't play to earn people's approval of our style."

Fratello said the hardest part about being fired by Cleveland was that he was never told why, other than the criticism about style of play.

"You understand that, in this profession, hiring and firing goes with the territory, especially when you lose," Fratello said. "But when you are in the playoffs almost every year, and you get fired, you're not quite sure what took place."

THE CZAR OF THE TELESTRATOR

Fratello had been in television before, joining NBC from 1990 to 1993 between his Atlanta and Cleveland coaching jobs. So when he returned to the airwaves after the Cavs fired him, he did so on TNT with Marv Albert, the NBA's quintessential play-by-play voice with whom Fratello had worked previously. They were ideal partners, meshing perfectly on and off the air, both armed with sharp senses of humor. Albert's nickname for Fratello "The Czar of the Telestrator" for Fratello's work diagramming plays electronically onscreen, introduced Fratello to a new generation of fans.

Even though Albert still calls Fratello "a walking punch line" and still can't resist zinging him from long-distance—"Tell the Czar to stay off the court. … He was so far out there one Grizzlies game I watched I thought he was setting a screen for Mike Miller," Albert once said—Albert knew that Fratello belonged back in coaching.

"Mike was everything you wanted in a color commentator—he knew his Xs and Os, he prepared, and he had a great sense of humor," Albert said. "But it was really absurd that he wasn't coaching. You saw people getting head coaching jobs that weren't as nearly as good as Mike. Yet, he never said a word about it."

Several hours after West called Fratello about the Grizzlies' job, after Albert and Fratello did the Thanksgiving TNT broadcast, they sat in a late-night joint in Indianapolis.

"Mike was wondering what he should do. He wanted to make sure it was the right situation," said Albert, who slips in and out of seriousness when talking about Fratello. "I knew he could always come back to television. I told him we would hate to lose him, but he had to do what he thought was right. Besides, I had gotten tired of sending out resumes and color photos of him to teams. There's not a day that goes by that we don't talk about him when we're doing a game. I get phone messages from him almost after every one of our games. He critiques us, whether he has seen the game or not. We really do miss him—he's a wonderful person. And I hate that he's going to see this in print."

MOLDING THE GRIZZLIES

When Fratello took over the Grizzlies, he found a team stunned by its slow start and reeling from Brown's sudden decision to quit. So he didn't do anything drastic, especially since he had 15 games in his first 27 days, with time for just three practices.

He took Brown's concepts and built on them. There were some subtle differences, like changing from Brown's motion offense to more pick-and-roll plays, as well as simplifying play-calling and tweaking Brown's strict 10-man rotation where everyone played a set amount of minutes.

"No matter how bad you were playing under Hubie, you were going to play your six-minute rotations," former Griz forward Shane Battier said. "Now with Coach [Fratello], if you're playing well, he'll keep you in there and keep calling plays for you. He recognizes mismatches and tries to exploit them. He feeds the machine, whoever the machine is at that moment. If you're not playing very well mentally, Coach will get you out of there. It has been an adjustment in terms of flow, but personally I enjoyed it. It makes you work harder to stay on the floor."

Some players adjusted easier than others to Fratello's style of substitution. "When you're dealing with a bunch of competitive people, they want to be out there and be out there as long as they can because they want to be a part of it," Fratello said. "I know that a player is going

In the Griz huddle, all eyes are on Mike Fratello.
© 2006 NBA Entertainment. Photo by Joe Murphy

to get bent out of shape in an 82-game season. It goes with the territory. You try to deal with it up front. You don't want it to come to a boiling point."

Despite the brief late-season turmoil and being swept in the first-round of the playoffs by the Suns, Fratello's first Griz team held a soft spot for him.

"I don't know if we reached our potential because of the injuries," Fratello said. "But what was great about that group is that with all the stuff going on—the slow start, the coaching change, new personalities, and some new offensive and defensive things—that they stayed competitive to keep themselves alive in the playoff race."

IT'S FRATELLO'S FAULT

There are those who love basketball Hall of Famer Bill Walton as an ESPN television analyst. ... And there are those who hate him. For those who don't like the big redhead, still somewhat of a love and peace hippie out of the late '60s and early '70s, blame Fratello.

"Mike was the person responsible for getting me into television, so I guess people will be looking to string Mike up," Walton said.

"No one wanted to hire a 6-foot-11 guy with red hair, big nose, freckles, and a speech impediment," Walton said. "Mike was doing color for the Clippers at the time in 1990, and he was willing to make a three-man crew instead of two. In a business known for egos and selfishness, I've never forgotten his generosity, his humility, and his willingness to share."

ONCE A FRIEND, ALWAYS A FRIEND

Fratello has never forgotten his New Jersey roots. Just ask Tony Karcich, one of Fratello's running buddies from their high school days in Hackensack. Karcich, the aforementioned football coach and athletic director at St. Joseph's Regional High in Montvale, New Jersey, recalled the time he guided his team to the state championship game at The Meadowlands in December 1995.

The last person he expected to see was his old pal Fratello, but …

"Mike just showed up outside the locker room," Karcich said. "So I asked him to come in and say a few words to the kids. He told them to cherish the moment, to feel good about what they accomplished. It was a nice speech. Then, we kickoff and the other team drove 80 yards for a touchdown. I was thinking, 'What kind of speech was that, Mike?' But it all worked out—we won. And later, it hit me: 'How can a guy who was coaching in the NBA take time in the season to come watch a high school football game?' That's Mike. He found the time."

13

MILLER TIME

THE SHOOTING MACHINE

The shot is so stunningly perfect that it should go in the basket every time: elbow in, shoulders square, straight jump, wrist cocked, follow through, picturesque rotation. The shot has been Mike Miller's calling card throughout his basketball career—both at the University of Florida, where his two-year stay resulted in an appearance in the 2000 NCAA finals against Michigan State, and in the NBA, where he has become one of the best long-range shooters in the game.

It's a shot that has been honed through years of practice. His stroke was better than ever in 2005-06, and one of the reasons is he finally achieved the dream of every kid who ever shot for hours in their backyard. At his home in the Memphis suburb of Collierville, Miller now has his own gym.

"I got up 500 or 600 shots a day in the summer," Miller said. "Sometimes, Mason [one of Miller's two sons] rebounds for me, though he likes to take his shots, too. A lot of times, I'll just go in there by myself. Sometimes I put on music; but a lot of times I just like to hear that ball bouncing and the sound the net makes when the ball goes through it."

There's nothing sweeter to Miller's ears. The 6-foot-8 swingman knows that's what his team needs from him. In 2004-05, the first time he was relatively healthy since he arrived in Memphis in a trade from Orlando midway through his third pro season in 2002-03, he showed the consistency everyone suspected had been bubbling under the surface. He averaged 13.4 points, shot a career-high 43.3 percent from three-point range, and began displaying an overall offensive game that opponents hadn't seen previously.

"Two years ago, before all of our eyes, we saw Mike grow as a player," Grizzlies coach Mike Fratello said. "At the end of the year, we not only saw a Mike Miller who could merely catch and shoot it—he could put it on the floor, create shots for his teammates, and finish at the basket. Along the way, he had some huge nights shooting the ball."

It was no surprise to Fratello, who calls Miller "the hardest working guy I've ever seen in the off-season … this guy loves the game."

Before '04-'05, some lingering questions arose as to whether the Grizzlies had traded for damaged goods when they got Miller in that trade a few years back. He played two games for the Griz before back spasms sidelined him in his home debut, and for the next one and a half seasons, he tried to play through the pain. But in the off-season two years ago, he did something about it. The strain on his back was because his playing weight was too heavy. It wasn't fat. Miller had made the mistake of muscling up too much in the weight room in previous off-seasons.

"I went through the same thing early in my career that Mike went through," said Grizzlies center Lorenzen Wright. "When you are trying to get in the league, people always tell you that you need to get bigger. I gained a lot of weight when I came into the league with the Clippers. But what you learn is that you play better at the size at which you are comfortable. When I lost that weight, I felt better. Mike has been trying to find out who he is in the NBA, and how to use his body. He's figured out what weight he needs to be."

The key was a 16-week off-season workout, planned by Grizzlies strength coach Mike Curtis. He designed a program that strengthened Miller's back and his core, including his abdomen. Miller didn't even blink at the four days per week, two hours per day workouts. Miller did a lot of conditioning in the swimming pool and mostly exercises using his own body weight.

"Mike didn't need to be bigger, he didn't need more muscle," Curtis said. "We wanted him slim, trim, and strong in the middle. We wanted him to be able to explode to the basket and be able to absorb blows—not get knocked out of whack."

And that's exactly how it played out. Miller's most serious injury in '04-'05 was a concussion. He played in 76 regular-season games—the most since he played the full 82 as a rookie at Orlando in 2000-01 when he was named the NBA's Rookie of the Year.

As '04-'05 progressed, Miller became increasingly aggressive. In the last month of the season, he averaged 18.7 points. He went for 30 points against the Heat, a career-high 37 on the Rockets, and 28 (including a game-winning 22-footer) against the Spurs.

"Mike was our most consistent player last year, bar none," former Grizzlies swingman Shane Battier said. "When he gets that jumper rolling, there's not much you can do about it."

In the playoffs against the Suns, Miller averaged 12 points and shot 47.1 percent from three-point land—a far cry from the 2004 playoffs against the Spurs, when he averaged 7.5 points and shot 38.3 percent in threes. Again, it all went back to his new body.

"Since I was hurt from start to finish my first couple of years here, it helps when you're healthy enough to get a little movement," Miller said. "The coaches have given me more scoring opportunities the last couple of seasons, putting me in a lot of pick-and-rolls."

Miller looks at his last two seasons as the natural maturation of his professional career. While his career started earlier than expected, jumping to the NBA after his sophomore season with the Gators, few days pass when he doesn't think about his time spent in Gainesville.

"It was a very tough decision to leave school," Miller said. "Had that [2000] team stayed together another year, I felt like we would have gone a long way again. But I had to do what was best for my family at the time, and Coach [Billy] Donavan understood that. When he recruited me, he understood what I wanted out of a college. He told me, 'After four years, if I don't have you ready for the NBA, then I haven't done my job.'"

Perhaps Miller wasn't ready when he left the Gators. However, Tony Barone, the player personnel director for the Grizzlies, held the same opinion other NBA teams did when Miller entered the draft and was chosen fifth overall by Orlando.

"If you're going to come out early, you need at least one NBA skill," Barone said. "The one thing that Mike brought to the table and allowed him to play right away in the NBA was his shooting ability."

TO THE HOOP

Miller's outside shot dramatically improved once he was able to develop a dribble-drive game.

"I used to always be like, 'I have to make shots,'" he said. "When you're a shooter, your conscience gets in the way. When you're a shooter, living on the outside instead of driving to the basket and getting to the free throw line like a scorer, you think every shot has to go in. Finally, I understood if I miss, I miss. Knowing that, as it relates to the game, is one of the best things that's ever happened to my game."

QUICK-CHANGE ARTIST

When Miller was traded from Orlando to the Grizzlies on February 19, 2003, he barely had time to pack a bag. After just one night of sleep, he flew to New Orleans to join the Grizzlies the next day for a game against the Hornets.

A physical and a crash course on the Griz playbook later, he scored a team-high 23 points in a 125-123 overtime loss.

"The coaching staff did a good job of going over plays with me, and I played on instinct," Miller said.

The crazy thing is, a few days later on the morning of the night that Miller was to make his Grizzlies home debut, he stubbed his toe on the floor in practice, causing his back to spasm, and tests revealed he sprained a back ligament. He had back problems the rest of the season.

BIRD WAS THE WORD

In a game where supreme athletes seem to dominate, Miller drew inspiration growing up from Celtics Hall of Famer Larry Bird, a 12-time

Griz swingman Mike Miller has textbook shooting form.
© 2006 NBA Entertainment. Photo by Layne Murdoch

all-star and three-time NBA Most Valuable Player. Liking Bird made sense to Miller. Miller was a 6-foot-8 country boy from a small South Dakota town who honed his outside shot to perfection to complement his inside skills. Bird was a 6-foot-9 Indiana country boy who played the game the same way.

"Bird did everything he possibly could to make his team better," Miller said. "He never forced many shots. Sometimes he'd have no points going into the fourth quarter and finish with 20. He could get a shot when he wanted. He could draw a foul when he wanted. He could make a great pass when he wanted. He's one of the few people to average 20 points, 10 rebounds, and six assists [23.8, 10.3, 6.5] for a career."

THE SIXTH MAN OF THE YEAR

As the '05-'06 season began, with the influx of new veterans, Griz coach Mike Fratello made a stunning move. He decided to take Miller out of the starting lineup and put him on the bench. The goal was to create instant offense.

"In my mind, Mike's a starter," Fratello said. "He plays just as many minutes as a starter. After the type of year he had last year, I wouldn't have blamed him this year if would have said, 'I'm outta here,' when I told him he would be coming off the bench. But he's not like that. He doesn't have any ego."

The move paid off. After averaging 13.7 points and 5.4 rebounds, Miller was named the league's Sixth Man of the Year. He became the only player in NBA history to win Rookie of the Year and the Sixth Man award.

"The situations I've gone through ever since I was a rookie taught me that you do what you can do with the minutes you're given," Miller said. "My job has been to go out there and give our team a boost, just do something to help us win. I get starter's minutes. When you sign a contract, it doesn't say that you're starting; it says that you're playing on the team. As long as I play on the team, I'm happy."

ONCE A GATOR, ALWAYS A GATOR

Miller enjoyed the '05-'06 season for many reasons. But when Florida made it to the NCAA championship game in Indianapolis and beat UCLA—the same game and place Miller played in 2000, when Florida lost in the finals to Michigan State—he couldn't have been prouder.

Miller still likes to wear his Florida practice shorts in the Griz locker room every so often. "I can tell these guys what it's like to be a Gator," he said.

Miller also talks to his college coach, Billy Donovan, several times each season. "I wanted them to win it, because I know how bad it felt to lose when we got there," Miller said. "I talked to Coach Donovan, and it's ironic it [was] in Indianapolis."

Miller loved Donovan from the first day they met during the recruiting process. How else can you explain a McDonald's All-American from Mitchell, South Dakota, ending up in Gainesville, Florida?

"It was Coach [Donovan]," Miller said. "You get a relationship with a guy, and it's important because that's the guy you'll be playing for the next four years. My relationship with Coach was it was good enough to draw me from South Dakota. He was like my father down there. He recruited me from the get-go, even when he was at Marshall before he went to Florida. I considered Kansas because it was in the Midwest. I also looked at Kentucky because I had family there. It was a tough decision, but I had confidence in what Coach Donovan was trying to do. It worked out well. The only thing Coach Donovan demands is that you play hard. You take shots when you're open, and sometimes you take shots when you're not open. Take a shot at the beginning or end of the shot clock. You have that freedom as long as you play hard."

In Miller's NCAA-championship loss to Michigan State, there were no regrets when it was over. The Gators, full of freshmen and sophomores, fell to a Spartans team dominated with upper classmen and several future NBA players.

"They had Zach Randolph, Mateen Cleaves, Morris Peterson, Jason Richardson. ... They had four pros on the team, and they were mature," Miller said. "They broke our press and made shots."

KUNG-FU KOBE

Miller got in Kobe Bryant's head in a 100-99 overtime win at Los Angeles on December 28, 2005. He cracked Bryant's noggin with his elbow during a third-quarter drive, so Bryant sought revenge.

Bryant was lucky he wasn't ejected from the game in the fourth quarter with an intentional elbow chop to Miller's throat. He was merely given a flagrant-foul penalty. Bryant was suspended for two games for his vicious elbow.

"Everyone's playing, and sometimes you question it," Miller said after the incident. "But we won, and that's the most important thing."

THE ROUND MOUND

Everybody expects Miller to hit threes or make aggressive drives. But nobody ever thought Miller would become a rebounding maniac, as he did several times during the '05-'06 season, such as his 16-rebound performance in an 81-69 win over the Nets in January.

Shane Battier called Miller "The Round Mound of Collierville" (the Memphis suburb where Miller lives) and Lorenzen Wright called Miller "the white Grant Hill" because of his suddenly steady all-around stat line. Miller said he was just doing his job.

"I'm just going to get the ball," Miller said. "I get rebounds any way I can. We focused at the beginning of the season that we needed to rebound better. It's one thing that has hurt us in the past. We've got to keep even the rebound battle."

"There must be a bonus in his contract," added Battier. "But the way Mike has rebounding the last few games is impressive for Ben Wallace, much less Mike Miller."

NEVER HOTTER

It doesn't matter how you start a game. It's how you finish, and Miller's finish against the Nuggets in a 116-102 victory in a March '06 game was one for the record books.

Miller scored a career-high 41 points, tying the franchise record held by Bryant "Big Country" Reeves. His 41 points, all off the bench, was the most in the league in the '05-'06 season by a player coming off the bench.

He became just the fourth player in team history to score 40 or more in a game. He set a team record for points in a game by a reserve, and tied a career-high with 15 field goals. He tied a season high for points in a half with 22 in the first, and tied another season high with 17 points in the fourth quarter.

"I got some good looks, and my teammates got me the ball," Miller said of his 15-of-24 shooting night.

HEAD GAMES

Miller's worst enemy may be himself. Even after he found the cure to his bad back, that didn't stop him from getting concussions. It seemed like his head was an elbow-seeking missile.

He nearly was knocked out by a screen from then-Hornets heavyweight forward Robert "Tractor" Traylor in an '04-'05 game. In the same season, after Griz teammate Lorenzen Wright knocked him silly with an accidental blow to the head, Miller said of his injury, "I just have a bad head."

14

HOME MAKEOVER, GRIZZLIES STYLE

DESTRUCTION AND RECONSTRUCTION

Majority owner Michael Heisley knew his team had to be re-modeled before the '05-'06 season, even if that meant losing Jason Williams and Bonzi Wells—two of his favorite players—to impending trades.

After all, business is business.

"As Jerry [West] said, 'We imploded a bit,'" Heisley said. "The pressure got to a couple of the players, two players that I happened to love as much as any on the team. I have deep affection for them, Jason and his family, as well as Bonzi. He'd call me 'Big Money' all the time; and I'd call him 'Small Change.' Almost every player that played for us, I still feel the same way toward them I've always felt. Nothing has changed with me. I talk to Mike Bibby every time I see him. It broke my heart when we traded Mike [to Sacramento for Jason Williams just before the Grizzlies moved to Memphis].

"I couldn't tell you anything that made me feel any better than to see one of our former guys, Tony Massenburg, win a championship ring with

Former Dodgers manager Tommy Lasorda enjoys a laugh with Jerry West, Mike Fratello, and West's son, Jonnie, at the California summer league.
© 2005 NBA Entertainment. Photo by Juan Ocampo

the Spurs," Heisley continued. "He really deserved it. He played hard and was a professional for many years."

The worst thing about being an owner to Heisley is losing, and "having so little control over whether you're going to win ... you can't buy a championship."

Heisley hasn't tried to be a flamboyant owner, like Mark Cuban in Dallas or the Maloofs in Sacramento. He likes to blend.

"I always said my ideal pro franchise for years was the Dallas Cowboys when they had Clint Murchison as owner, Tex Schramm as general manager, and Tom Landry as the coach," Heisley said. "I thought Landry coached the team, Schramm went out and got the players; and Murchison was the owner who kept in background.

"That's the way I want to be. My job was to go get Jerry West [as president of basketball operations], and Jerry West's job is to do the other things," Heisley said. "I don't trade players, and I don't hire them. That's

Jerry's job. My job is to give Jerry the tools to do his job. I'm not going to kid myself—I got opinions. I sit there and cuss. But I recognize I couldn't even make my starting team in basketball in high school, so I don't think I'm as good as Jerry West. I got one of the best, so I let Jerry do his job. I give him all the support that I can give him."

For Heisley, philanthropy was a major objective as an owner. He wanted to be able to do things that one normally couldn't do alone. "I know it isn't the Grizzlies, but when I was driving to the arena today, the city of Memphis looks a lot better and a lot healthier since we came here," Heisley said. "All I'm saying is that the mayor and everybody ought to be proud. If you step back and see where we were four years ago and see what we have today, you see a city on the move."

Heisley had a feel for the Memphis community even before he grew interested in moving his team from Vancouver.

"My father worked on the Southern Railway, which came through Memphis," Heisley said. "I grew up in the south, and I knew Memphis has a great music tradition. I knew that it had a vibrant black community, and that FedEx was here. As I got more involved, this turned out to be a great relationship."

BLAZING A TRAIL TO MEMPHIS

After eight seasons in Portland, point guard Damon Stoudamire needed a change of scenery. When he began looking around as a free agent in the summer of 2005, the thought of being a veteran leader of an up-and-coming playoff team suddenly appealed to him.

"I'd been in the same place for eight years," Stoudamire said. "You just need a change. It was definitely good for me to be involved with a new organization and a new coach. By staying in the same place, I kind of forgot how the rest of the NBA worked. When you've been somewhere for so long, you get taken for granted. I think people forget what you brought to a team and you do, too. So, when you go to a new team, you kind of remember again because people start telling you what you can bring to a team. It was refreshing coming here to Memphis."

Immediately, Stoudamire established the steady, "pass first, shoot second" point guard the Grizzlies had sought forever. He increasingly

Damon Stoudamire brought fire and leadership to the Griz backcourt.
© 2005 NBA Entertainment. Photo by Fernando Medina

showed in his first month on the job that, although he may struggle shooting early, he was absolutely clutch late in games.

"When it comes to me in those situations I want to take the shot," Stoudamire said. "Coming down to the last two minutes, I want the ball. My teammates believe in me down the stretch. They look for me. I just tell the guys sometimes it doesn't matter if you're 0-for-the-field. You have to shoot those shots with confidence."

That alone was enough for the Griz fans to take to him.

"The biggest thing I like is the influence I have with the guys on this team," Stoudamire said. "I think they all understand that I know the game, and I've been through a lot of stuff they're trying to [accomplish]. I haven't been to the NBA Finals, but I've come as close as anybody in this locker room—Coach Fratello included."

That's why the Grizzlies spiraled into a brief nosedive after Stoudamire was sidelined for the season, sustaining a torn patella tendon on a drive to the basket after just 27 games in a Griz uniform. After surgery, instead moping about the first season-ending injury of his career, Stoudamire made sure to continue his role as a leader. As soon as he was able, he was on crutches and back at FedExForum supporting his teammates.

"I decided a long time ago that, for me to make it in the league, that I had to be a tough-minded person," Stoudamire said. "This injury is just another obstacle for me, and I'm tough enough to handle it. The moment I got hurt, when I was up in the air before I even hit the floor, my mind was already working. It was like, '[This is] going to be something I'm going to have to get through. I don't know what it is yet, but it's something.' The first thing I told myself when I got hurt is, 'I've got to be strong for everybody on this team. I had to let everybody know I was going to be alright.'"

STEADY EDDIE

Unruffled Eddie Jones was the steady voice of reason through the 2005-06. He never got too high after a victory and never too low after a loss.

"One thing about veterans is, we know you're going to have bad stretches during the season," Jones said. "During those bad stretches, you have to continue to pat each other on the back and work harder. Having veterans who have true professionalism helps teams go a long way."

His teammates appreciated him.

"Eddie is always trying to keep the morale up, he just looks out for everybody," Griz center Lorenzen Wright said. "He's a real veteran. We've never had that on this team."

Every once in a while, Jones' old legs got tired. In a 10-point win over the Clippers in late March '06, Jones had a breakaway dunk late in the game. But his tired legs simply gave out. He laid in a reverse drive and was greeted from snickers and laughs from the entire Griz bench.

"Even the coaches were laughing at me," Jones said. "They must have forgotten the dunk I had against the Timberwolves a few weeks [earlier]."

VETERAN LEADERSHIP

A year removed from the Grizzlies' season-ending collapse, fueled mostly by two veterans angered over their roles, the '05-'06 Griz were a shining example of how a team can create a positive locker room with some personnel changes.

"I see happy people on this team, who are excited to come to work and be a part of this team, working together to get somewhere," said Griz all-star forward Pau Gasol, just before the start of the playoffs. "I don't see selfish guys who are worrying about themselves and their situations. We have guys happy to share and doing whatever it takes to win. That is what we've lacked in previous years."

The subtraction of malcontents like Jason Williams and Bonzi Wells (traded to Miami and Sacramento respectively), and the additions of veterans Eddie Jones, Bobby Jackson, Damon Stoudamire, and Chucky Atkins provided unerring professionalism.

"The balance in this league is such a delicate thing," Grizzlies coach Mike Fratello said. "Unless you're overwhelming on your roster one-through-12 deep, there are certain things that are the difference in being successful or not. One is injury. The other is having the right balance in your locker room, which allows you to go through such a stretch where we had 12 losses in 15 games. At that point, do you fall apart and start pointing fingers? Or do you hang in there and re-group?"

But the Grizzlies sailed through every potential situation where bruised egos could have ignited a firestorm.

"But it's all about being professional, it's maturity," explained veteran guard Bobby Jackson. "You learn your role, the way they use you; and you make the best of your time out there."

Atkins understands Jackson's points. It's no accident they have lockers next to each other in the FedExForum, a couple of veterans who have seen good and bad locker-room karma.

"When you've got a situation where guys aren't getting along, you just keep basically keep your mouth closed and go about your business," Atkins said. "That's about all you can do. But look around [the Grizzlies' locker room]—guys are sitting around, talking, and laughing. You don't see a lot of that in this league, especially guys that play the same position. When guys get along, that can carry you sometimes."

For hometown-favorite Lorenzen Wright, swallowing his ego was no easy task; yet he played his most effective basketball of his career from the bench.

"To be a professional, sometimes you've got to put aside how you are playing or the number of minutes you're playing, you have to check it at the door and just come to win," Wright said. "That's what everybody has on their minds, winning games. It's harder when you have to fight attitudes on your own team and then have to fight the other team. If one person is unhappy, then everybody is unhappy."

Most of the Grizzlies credit the cool Jones—the 12-year veteran who had previously played for the Lakers, Charlotte, and Miami—for keeping the locker room tranquil.

"You make jokes, you make sure you stay together even if things aren't going great on the floor," Jones said. "You stay positive, and not let anybody stray away from each other. You encourage and you focus on what's next. I played for Miami last year, and the reason we clicked is because everybody was together in the locker room. I know how far that can take you. We're [the Grizzlies] one of the most unselfish teams in the league. We really do enjoy each other and that transfers to the floor."

One of the big surprises of the '05-'06 season was the vast improvement of Griz center Jake Tsakalidis. © 2006 NBA Entertainment. Photo by Nikki Boertman

BEHOLD BIG JAKE

The unexpected development of backup center Jake Tsakalidis in the last half of the '05-'06 season was one of the nicest surprises of the year. Grizzlies coach Mike Fratello said he was pleased because Tsakalidis took inside pressure off Pau Gasol.

"You're seeing teams make the decision to run a second defender at Pau, and he's an unselfish player," Fratello said. "It's going to find open teammates, and it's a matter of them hitting shots. Hopefully, Jake will keep playing well enough where defenses can't afford to help, that they'll play Pau with one guy. Jake gets most of his points and rebounds from hard work, effort and being in the right place at the right time. He always finds open seams in a defense where someone can get him a pass."

"The more I play, the more I get in game shape," Tsakalidis said. "I just feel better, feel like I can finish around the basket. I've tried to keep in shape when I wasn't playing, but it's not the same as playing in a game."

0-FOR-FOREVER IN THE PLAYOFFS

When the Grizzlies went four-and-out in the playoffs for the third straight season—the 12-consecutive playoff losses an NBA record—all the good will of a 49-win regular season quickly vanished.

"We played a great team [the Mavs], but we've been here in the playoffs a couple of years now," Grizzlies' guard Mike Miller said. "We came in this series hoping to steal one, because we came in playing well down the stretch."

Nobody hurt more that Grizzlies' president, Jerry West. Not only had he seen the team he put together fold again in the playoffs, but he saw the Grizzlies' fans begin to turn on their team. Whether it was being swept again, or fans showing displeasure over the team's deliberate style of offense, it was clear to West that, in looking ahead to the '06-'07 season, things needed to be shaken up again.

"Winning games in this league for me is never enough," West said a couple of days after the season ended. "Somewhere along the way, we've disconnected with our fans. People in this town like basketball, and they're sophisticated. Somewhere along the way, we're going to have to do some things different around here. Michael Heisley [majority owner] and our minority owners have allowed us at great expense to get players who we think will help us win. That simply has to stop. You can't keep doing that. The amount of money lost here [more than $40 million, according to *The Commercial Appeal*], we shouldn't even be talking about. If these players can't get it done when it counts, maybe we need to start over. That's not something I recommend, because that's a painful process.

"We need our better players to play like better players," West continued. "We need to stop praising their opponents and look in the mirror, as I've been doing. I question myself more than I do the players. The burden falls on me, and obviously I'm not doing something right. But we need to do something different, that's for sure. Teams have players or a player who refuses to let them lose. We need to find that player, or our younger players have to develop that attitude. Every loose ball, we have it to run down. Every time there's a free throw, we need to block out. This is what we need to do to take the next step.

"To our fans, please don't give up on us," West requested. "We're going to do everything we can this summer to make this team better, knowing we have to watch the dollars we spent around here more carefully. It won't be from a lack of trying on our part upstairs. Last year, we imploded. This year, we didn't do the little things necessary to win [playoff] games. We picked a very poor time not to play at a high level. Our better players didn't play at a high level. If I owned this team, I'd say, 'Don't spend a penny. The losses here are enormous.' We have a great owner and great ownership, and they won't let that happen. But if I owned the team, it would be completely different."

The problems that West saw with the Grizzlies in the playoffs were nothing new.

"Our problems all year have been rebounding and free-throw shooting," West said. "If we would have made another free throw [in the final minute of Game 3], we wouldn't have lost that game. Would that have changed the complexion of the series? I don't know that. But there would have been more pressure on them [the Mavs] that last game. They were laughing at us. I don't like to be laughed at."

Pau Gasol, the team's centerpiece, promised he'd come back with a vengeance.

"I need to be more dominant and a force," Gasol said. "I need to be more selfish. I think I am the guy that everybody counts on. But it would be nice to have somebody else inside to have a presence, to be able to intimidate and not be dominated. That would help us in the playoffs, when every team comes to play."

15

IF YOU MUST KNOW...

n their five seasons in Memphis, the Grizzlies have had an assortment of players with the courage to tackle a wide range of topics:

WHY DID YOU PICK THE JERSEY NUMBER YOU WEAR?

Mike Miller (No. 33): "Larry Legend [Bird]. He and Michael Jordan were my two favorite players. I loved the things that Larry did—not just scoring but everything. He made people around him better, and I try to make people around me have an easier night."

Jason Williams (No. 2): "The most favorite jersey number I wore was No. 55 at the University of Marshall. I liked it because it was different. When I was a freshman at Marshall, we started three guards. One wore 50, one wore 52, and I wore 55. I loved 55."

Lorenzen Wright (No. 42): "My Dad wore that number. He didn't know I was going to get it. It was a big man's number. My Dad wore Nos. 42, 6, and 9, but I liked that big man's number. I decided when I got big enough, I was going to get a big man's number. I got No. 42 and stuck with it."

Chucky Atkins (No. 32): "I've been on three teams in two years, so I got 32."

Eddie Jones (No. 6): "Dr. J, Julius Erving wore it. That's it."

Damon Stoudamire (No. 20): "I grew up a Gary Payton fan. We'd known each other since like the 10th grade."

Pau Gasol (No. 16): "That's the number I was given when I was 18 years old and I first played for the professional team in Barcelona. Those are the numbers they gave to the junior players on the team. The numbers go from No. 4 to No. 15, and then they have No. 16 and No. 17 for the younger players. I got No. 16 and played great with it, so I kept it. I didn't want any of the numbers between four and 15."

WHAT'S THE WORST THING YOU DID AS A CHILD?

Earl Watson: "A lot of times when I was a kid in Kansas City, all my older brothers would be at work when I came home from school. So I'd make my younger sister play me one-on-one. One time, my sister had a lead, it was almost game point, and there was a loose ball. So we were outside, it was cold; and it had rained. She's about to get that loose ball and score, so I aggressively attacked the ball and pushed her off into the mud. I got the ball and scored. That's the last time we played one-on-one. She never played against me again. She went and told my mom, and I got in trouble."

James Posey: "Oh, man. Maybe the dumbest thing I did was jumping from the second story of abandoned building on to a couple of mattresses. I did it just for fun. I didn't get hurt. Long as you landed on both mattresses, you were fine."

Bonzi Wells: "I busted a big K-Mart picture window by throwing a rock at it. I was a bad little boy hanging with a bunch of older cats. I was always the youngest. They basically told me, 'Bonzi, break the window, do it!' I was stupid. My dad heard about it, and I got in a little bit of trouble."

Shane Battier: "When I was about four years old, I threw a one-man surprise party for myself and invisible friends. I took every sock, piece of underwear, every T-shirt, out of my drawers, dumped them on the floor, and dumped a whole can of baby powder all over the room. I think my behind is still scarred from the punishment."

Chucky Atkins: "I accidentally shot one of my cousins with a BB gun. I got really scared."

Damon Stoudamire: "I used to steal money from my grandmother to go play video games. She didn't whip me, but my mother whipped me for it."

WHO'S YOUR TOUGHEST MATCHUP IN THE LEAGUE?

Earl Watson: "Baron Davis [of the Warriors], because we work out with each other so much in the summer. We know each other's games so well that it's a chess game when we play. We know what's going to come next, but we don't know when it's coming. It's real competitive when we play. We both wish each other the best, but we both want to take our games to the next level when we play."

James Posey: "Anybody that shoots the ball a lot … someone who is the focal point of the offense. Those guys are tough. Everybody tries to get those guys open to get their shots."

Bonzi Wells: "When I first got in the league, it was Kobe [Bryant], and it still is. He can do so much with the ball. He demands double teams; he can shoot outside; he can take you off the dribble; and he can take you down low."

Shane Battier: "I'd say a guy like Tracy McGrady or a Kobe Bryant, somebody who can do it all. You never know how they are going to try and score on you."

Chucky Atkins: "I'd say Jason Kidd or Chauncey Billups, physical guards who can shoot from the outside."

Eddie Jones: "He's not in the league anymore, but it was Mitch Richmond."

Damon Stoudamire: "It's Allen Iverson. He's got the green light, and he's in attack mode. There's no other guard in this league who's in an attack mode from start to finish."

WHAT'S THE CLOSEST THING YOU HAVE TO A HOBBY?

Lorenzen Wright: "I began hunting. I always wanted to go hunting. When I was a kid growing up in Mississippi, all my friends went hunting, but I'd never been hunting. I told the Reverend Bill Adkins that, and he's a real big hunter. One day he called me, we drove up to Oklahoma where they have one of those big hunting ranges. I shot me a buffalo. We're still eating some of that meat."

Earl Watson: "I like to do a lot of different things. During the season, it's hard for me to do anything because I like to rest a lot. I talk to my family a lot … keep in contact with them. I also watch a lot of movies."

James Posey: "Bowling—in my spare time, I get out on my own. I have my own ball, shoes, and bag. I'm serious."

Bonzi Wells: "Video games—that's all I do. If I'm not playing basketball, I'm playing video games. That's what I love to do. Basketball used to be my hobby, but it became my profession. Now, it's video games. I'm good at football, basketball, baseball, NASCAR, video poker—I've got $575 million in the bank. So I'm doing well."

Shane Battier: "Playing the guitar—when I have some free time, I devote it to getting better at playing the guitar. I've come a long way. I can actually play a few songs now, like some Hootie and the Blowfish. My best one is probably 'Hey Joe' by Jimi Hendrix."

Brian Cardinal: "I play golf, and I'm taking some guitar lessons. I'm learning a little bit on guitar from Shane. He is pretty good. I like golf just to go out and hack around with some of my friends, just relaxing and having a good time."

Eddie Jones: "I play poker."

Damon Stoudamire: "Shopping for clothes—I really like clothes."

WHAT'S YOUR FAVORITE ALL-TIME MOVIE?

Lorenzen Wright: "Any of the Sylvester Stallone movies, like all the *Rocky* movies and *Rambo*. I loved the *Rocky* movies. I remember when I was a kid and watching a trailer on television of the latest *Rocky* movie. I'd just cry, 'I want to go see the new *Rocky*.'"

Mike Miller: "I like a lot of them, but *The Shawshank Redemption* is a great movie. Just what the main character did to get out of prison, he was a pretty smart man."

Brian Cardinal: "*Tommy Boy* with Chris Farley. It was one of those funny, stupid movies. I like some of his other movies, like *Black Sheep*. He was a piece of work."

Earl Watson: "There are so many good movies out there. A classic I like is *The Outsiders*, when Ralph Macchio and Patrick Swayze were just young kids. It's funny how young they look, and they don't look like they've aged until this day."

James Posey: "*Scarface*—You can feel the pain of those gangster flicks because they're so intense."

Bonzi Wells: "*The Shawshank Redemption*—There's something about that movie, that the guy is down, he's going through all that adversity, but he still came out on top, he still rose above it. It's an inspirational movie for me. You can take a little lesson from that movie."

Shane Battier: "*Old School*—it's great."

Dahntay Jones: "*The Five Heartbeats*—a story about a singing group. It's a classic."

Ryan Humphrey: "That [TV] movie on The Temptations and *The Godfather*. I like all those Mafia movies."

Stromile Swift: "I like *Life* with Eddie Murphy and Martin Lawrence. I like all those comedies."

Antonio Burks: "*Home Alone*. I still love *Home Alone*. I first saw it when I was 12 or 13 years old. They kept on making sequels, and they were all funny; but I liked the first one the best."

Damon Stoudamire: "*Scarface*."

IF YOU WEREN'T IN THE NBA,
WHAT WOULD YOU BE DOING?

Lorenzen Wright: "I'd be coaching. I got it from Dad, who was a coach. I watched him, I learned from him. I really like the idea of coaching kids. It's something I want to do after I retire."

Brian Cardinal: "I'd be on a farm back in Illinois, hanging loose and waking up every day looking forward to the new day. I worked on farms before in the summertime. I can see myself after my NBA career getting some acreage and relaxing. I don't know if I know enough about farming to go full-blown into it."

Mike Miller: "I'd probably be coaching. I'd try to do that anyway."

Dahntay Jones: "I'd be in grad school, working toward a career in finance and investments."

Antonio Burks: "I'd still be in school finishing my degree."

Earl Watson: "I'd probably be affiliated in sports somehow. I'd want to help kids, but at the same time have challenges every day to where I have a chance to overcome them. My game is versatile, and I think I'll be versatile in life. I think the way you play is a reflection of your life and how you handle yourself as a person. The game and life are so parallel, it's unbelievable."

James Posey: "I'd be doing something with forensic science. It's something that got my attention in school. I like that challenge. It's like putting pieces of a puzzle together. You start off with nothing, but you put a whole case together."

Bonzi Wells: "I wonder about that all the time. I came from Indiana, so basketball is about the only thing I've ever done. In Indiana, basketball is your life."

Shane Battier: "I would be working with the kids in some capacity, as a coach or a teacher or a mentor. I want to give back and be taught the way I was taught when I was young."

Ryan Humphrey: "I'd be in the NFL [Humphrey was a *Parade* All-American at Tulsa (Oklahoma) Booker T. Washington]. I was a tight end. I think about it sometimes why I chose basketball over football. But I'm here now, and I can't complain."

If Griz forward Brian Cardinal wasn't playing in the NBA, he'd be chillin' on a farm back in his home state of Illinois. © 2006 NBA Entertainment. Photo by Joe Murphy

Stromile Swift: "I went to school in sports medicine and kinesiology, so I'd probably be a personal trainer or something in that area."

Chucky Atkins "I'd be a computer programmer. I love computers."

Eddie Jones: "I'd be trying to become a professional poker player."

Damon Stoudamire: "Probably something in television production … I majored in media arts and broadcasting in college. I grew up watching television, and when I got to college, I wanted something that I wasn't going to be bored with. I took a couple of journalism classes, but I didn't like those deadlines. I couldn't make those. I like the whole aspect of production … the cameras, everything."

WHAT PLAYER(S) GETS THE MOST FAVORABLE OFFICIATING CALLS?

Lorenzen Wright: "Referees are human. They watch television just like we watch television. If you're a ref out there and see a superstar coming in against somebody's who not a superstar, you're going to give them the benefit of the doubt just because you've seen them on television, and that's what's supposed to happen. I think they try to keep it as even as possible, and I don't think they try to help certain teams win. They try to do it as even as humanly possible."

Earl Watson: "I used to think that. My first couple of years here with the Grizzlies, I thought every team we played got a lot of calls. We hardly got any calls. After Hubie [Brown] came [as coach], we had some success and won 50 games, I think it's pretty fair. You get respect [from officials]. It's all about growing pains and paying your dues as an organization. Older guys should get the majority of the calls because they've been in the league. Younger players have to work to get to that point."

Mike Miller: "The best players have the ball so much of the time, and they do so much, that the refs expect what they do. I don't think it's favorable calls—the refs are just used to seeing those players do those things. They aren't used to seeing other guys do it, and you may not get the calls sometimes."

Bonzi Wells: "Every team has a superstar. T-Mac, Kobe, Shaq, Tim Duncan, KG, all those guys they know how to make you foul them. I don't know if they get the calls, but they know how to make a play to put the referee in a position where they have to call something. That's what superstars do well."

Shane Battier: "The all-star players get the calls. They have the ball in their hands. The more aggressive you are with the basketball, the more calls you're going to get. That's just the way it is."

Dahntay Jones: "I don't see that. Some guys work so hard that they deserve them. The referees recognize how hard those players work and how much contact they draw. Maybe you saw someone like Michael Jordan get calls all the time, but there's nobody like that now."

Ryan Humphrey: "All-stars get the calls because they get beat up a lot."

WHO'S THE TOUGHEST PLAYER YOU PLAYED AGAINST IN COLLEGE?

Brian Cardinal (Purdue): "Raef LaFrentz and Paul Pierce of Kansas. Those guys were awesome players, and both were tough to guard. I guarded LaFrentz. He was a beast back then and still is now."

Earl Watson (UCLA): "Probably Mike Bibby [of Arizona]. He was so complete. The guy would never say a word. But before you knew it, he had 18 points and nine assists. He did in such a professional way. He was real efficient with his shot in the time he got to play."

Lorenzen Wright (Memphis): "Danny Fortson of Cincinnati. It was a big challenge for me, very tough to guard."

Bonzi Wells (Ball State): "Gary Trent of Ohio played in my conference [the MAC], and he was called the 'Shaq of the Maq.' He was so aggressive, and he dunked on everybody. Sometimes, he played my position, so I had to guard him. It was crazy."

Shane Battier (Duke): "It would probably be Elton Brand, my teammate. I had him every day in practice."

Mike Miller (Florida): "Probably against Morris Peterson of Michigan State in the NCAA championship game. He was unbelievable. What he did in the championship game against us proved he was a great player. He made a lot of shots after they broke our press."

Antonio Burks (Memphis): "Steve Logan [of Cincinnati]. He was an offensive threat who could shoot threes; but he could also drive, get into your body and create fouls."

Dahntay Jones (Rutgers, Duke): "Besides my own teammates, me and Josh Howard of Wake Forest went at it a lot. There were some heated games in which we both fouled out. He competes so hard and moves around so much."

Ryan Humphrey (Oklahoma, Notre Dame): "I was in the Big 12 with Paul Pierce and Raef Lafrentz [both from Kansas] and Marcus Fizer of Iowa State. The Big East had some good players, too."

Stromile Swift (LSU): "Dan Langhi of Vanderbilt was the toughest. He was so hard to guard. They ran him off a lot of screens, and our big guys wouldn't come off the screens quick enough to help defensively. You don't see a lot of big guys like Langhi go out and shoot on the perimeter."

Eddie Jones (Temple): "Abdul Fox of Rhode Island. He was a beast."

Damon Stoudamire (Arizona): "It was J-Kidd [Jason Kidd of California]. He was so big and physical. The way he is now is the way he was his freshman year."

WHO'S THE BEST DUNKER IN THE NBA?

Lorenzen Wright: "Vince Carter, easy—he's the best dunker ever."

Earl Watson: "I'd say Amare Stoudemire. He comes with everything in the paint."

Antonio Burks: "I'd have to go with LeBron James, because he's creative. I like Amare Stoudemire, too, because he brings power."

Bonzi Wells: "It's tough because of all these young boys coming through the league, like Atlanta's Josh Smith [the dunk contest winner], Tony Allen of Boston, J.R. Smith of New Orleans, all those young boys besides the LeBrons and Dwyane Wades. They all got those young legs."

Shane Battier: "Josh Smith—that kid is pretty good."

Mike Miller: "Vince Carter—when he had his opportunity in the dunk contest several years ago, he did dunks that no one else could do. He's one of the best athletes you'll ever see."

James Posey: "For game situations, you've got to go with Vince Carter. He can do nearly anything in the flow of the game. Very few people have done in a game that they will do in a dunk contest. Vince has done it all."

Dahntay Jones: "Vince Carter, by far—he has size, creativity, and he does stuff you see in dunk contests during the course of a game."

Ryan Humphrey: "That's tough, because each time has some leapers. It's probably Josh Smith, who won the dunk contest once."

Stromile Swift: "It's Vince Carter, hands down. If you play pickup [games] with him, he has so much creativity, so much other stuff that people haven't seen. If he got in the dunk contest again, he'd win it easy."

Brian Cardinal: "Amare Stoudemire—he's got a lot of power. I also like Jason Richardson."

Chucky Atkins: "Vince Carter—no one is in second."

Eddie Jones: "Vince Carter, by far."

Damon Stoudamire: "It's Vince Carter. It has been Vince Carter for a long time, but everybody has been mad at him for some reason."

IF YOU COULD HAVE DINNER WITH ANY NBA LEGEND, LIVING OR DEAD, WHO WOULD IT BE AND WHAT WOULD YOU ASK HIM?

Lorenzen Wright: "[Celtics center] Bill Russell. I'd ask him how it was playing back then, because it had to be hard. I want to ask him if winning his 10th NBA championship ring felt the same as winning his first ring."

Earl Watson: "It's hard because I've been lucky to have relationships with guys I've looked up to, such as Magic Johnson and Jerry West. I met Michael Jordan when I was younger. Every time I saw Magic, I asked him a lot of questions when I trained with him in the summers. I'd get a chance to talk to Jerry when he was with the Lakers. And there was also [legendary former UCLA] Coach [John] Wooden sitting right behind our bench."

Bonzi Wells: "Growing up in Indiana, Michael Jordan and Scottie Pippen were my favorite players. When I played in Portland, I got a chance to play on the same team as Scottie. Scottie was my guy; I always wanted to play his game. When I first saw him as a teammate, I couldn't even breathe. He took me under his wing and showed me a lot about life on and off the court. Meeting your idol is one thing. Meeting them *and* getting a chance to play with them is a whole 'nother thing. I was blessed."

Shane Battier: "I would sit down with Bill Russell. He's done what everyone is trying to do, and that's become a champion—and he has done it 10 times. I'd see what his mind-set is and how he reached a level of consistency that is unparalleled in sports."

Mike Miller: "It would be with Larry Bird and Michael Jordan. I'd ask Larry about the things he did to get himself better. He wasn't overly athletic, but he continued to improve and win. I'd just ask Jordan about everything."

James Posey: "I'll take my chances and have dinner with the top-50 greatest players. I'm sure I'd learn a bit of something from each of them."

Dahntay Jones: "Michael Jordan. I'd ask him when and where and how did his career take off in leaps and bounds, how did it all develop, what he did [to get there]."

Ryan Humphrey: "Somebody like Bill Russell, who has done a lot of other things besides basketball. You can learn a lot from him."

Stromile Swift: "It would probably be Bernard King. I'd want to know how he maintained at such a high level when there was a lot of negative stuff going on around him. He kept his focus and played well as one of the greatest players to play the game."

Brian Cardinal: "Larry Bird. We'd just talk. Nothing in particular. I'd just want to know what made him be the best."

Chucky Atkins: "Michael Jordan. I want to pick his brain."

Eddie Jones: "Pete Maravich. He was crazy, but I loved him."

Damon Stoudamire: "It would be Nate Archibald, and only because I grew up liking him. I caught him late in his career, but he was left-handed and I'm left-handed. I get compared to him, so I'd love to talk to him."

WHAT PERSON WOULD YOU LIKE TO TRADE SPOTS WITH FOR A DAY?

Lorenzen Wright: "It would be Bill Gates. I just want one day as him to spend every dime he's got."

Earl Watson: "No one. Never change places with anyone."

Bonzi Wells: "Jay-Z. If I could be with Jay-Z for one day, and be with Beyonce (Jay-Z's girlfriend) and still rap, and make millions, that would be great. Beyonce is more of a prize than the rapping."

James Posey: "No one. I'm happy being myself."

Shane Battier: "I want to trade with Shaq (Heat center Shaquille O'Neal), just from the standpoint I get pushed around a lot, and I'm not the strongest guy. If I could just go out and push people around and beat them, and be stronger than anyone else on the court for just one day, that's all I ask. I wouldn't even have to score. I don't have to do anything but be strong. I'd be happy with that."

Dahntay Jones: "Nobody. I'm quite content with who I am. I enjoy my life. I'm blessed."

Mike Miller: "Tiger Woods, because I'd like to see how it felt to hit golf balls the way he does. Anyone that plays golf would want to do that for a day."

Stromile Swift: "I like to be reminded where I come from, so I'd trade places with a normal 9-to-5 working person. It would remind me to be grateful for what I have and the things I'm able to do."

Ryan Humphrey: "I'm happy where I'm at."

Brian Cardinal: "Maybe the President (Bush), just to see what the job is all about. I'd like one of his low-key days, like when he's at Camp David, or playing golf, or riding around in his helicopter."

Eddie Jones: "My wife. Being the wife of an NBA player, she has to deal with my travel and taking care of the kids. I'd like to see what that's like."

WHAT VACATION SPOT HAVE YOU ALWAYS WANTED TO VISIT?

Lorenzen Wright: "I've been to Paris, because we went in the preseason one year. But it was a business trip and we never left the hotel. I want to go to Paris with my wife. Usually when we go on vacation, it's with the kids."

Earl Watson: "I've heard a lot of great things about Europe. I've been to Paris and Spain, so I'd like to go to London and Italy."

Bonzi Wells: "Growing up, when I looked at maps I always say the Virgin Islands. I always thought it sounded funny, but it's a place where I always wanted to go."

Shane Battier: "I'd like to go to Tahiti."

Mike Miller: "I've always wanted to go to Africa. I'm intrigued by animals."

James Posey: "If I can't catch the Greyhound as a last resort, then I don't need to be there. We went overseas one preseason, and I had to go. I don't mind flying. But I want to get there and back. I'd rather take the Greyhound."

Dahntay Jones: "I want to go to the south of France. Just relax on the beach. I've heard it's very beautiful."

Stromile Swift: "Any island where there is clear blue water. When I was younger, I wanted to go Hawaii. Once I got to Hawaii, I went to Honolulu. It was nice, but it wasn't the island I wanted to go to. I want to go somewhere more exotic."

Brian Cardinal: "Mexico. Never been to Mexico, and someday I'll go."

Chucky Atkins: "Brazil, because of the women."

Eddie Jones: "I've already been everywhere."

Damon Stoudamire: "Fiji. And I'm going there this summer (of '06)."

NAMETAGS, PLEASE.

When Pau Gasol enters the Griz locker room for the '06-'07 season, perhaps it will hit him. Shane Battier is no longer in the corner to his left, traded to Houston. Lorenzen Wright, who wasn't offered a new contract with the Grizzlies and was expected to sign with Atlanta, is no longer to his right.

Gasol is the last man standing. He is the only player left on the Grizzlies that has been with the team since it moved from Memphis. It's not as if he knew changes weren't coming. Status quo can't maintain year-to-year appearances in the playoffs.

"I don't know what else I can do to help us win in the playoffs," Gasol said two days after the Griz were swept by the Mavs in the Western Conference first round. "It would be nice to have a bigger presence inside. …You can win games in the regular season, because you might catch a team that's tired. But in the playoffs, everybody plays hard."

Griz President Jerry West took note and got two long, 6-foot-9 athletic bodies in the draft—selecting Connecticut's Rudy Gay in a first-round trade with Houston, and getting Florida State's Alexander Johnson in a second-round trade with Portland. Throw in the Griz's original first-round draft choice, Villanova point guard Kyle Lowry, and West was giddy over his rookies, especially after how well they played in the California summer league.

"We felt the most talented player in the draft was Rudy Gay," West said. "And Alexander Johnson is one of the toughest, hardest-working kids I have seen in a long time. There was somebody taken real high in the draft [for whom] I would not trade this kid—we think we got a steal. We wanted to draft him in the first round, that's how much we thought of him. This is an extraordinary young man, a physical, rebounding force.

"We brought Kyle in for an interview before the draft, and he's one of the most charming kids I've ever met," West continued. "But watch him play—he's one tough kid. If there's a loose ball, he's going to get it. He's going to help us play at a different level from where we're at now."

Gay was promoted all summer on the Griz website. Anyone logging in would be greeted with a slideshow and the chant "Rudy, Rudy, Rudy" taken from the movie soundtrack "Rudy," the story of a Notre Dame football walk-on.

The team also decided to sell a block of season tickets at $5 per game, the lowest ticket price in the NBA. Yes, the Griz are trying to everything possible to get better.

It all starts with that first playoff win.

When it happens, wherever they are, Shane Battier and Lorenzen Wright, amongst all the other names and faces who contributed to thehistory of the Grizzlies, will still be smiling.

Celebrate the Heroes of Tennessee and American Sports
in These Other NEW and Recent Releases from Sports Publishing!

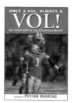

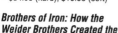
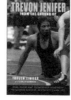